Airline
Flee
(Second E

Alan J. Wright

IAN ALLAN
Publishing

PREFACE

Since the first edition of this book was published there have been a considerable number of changes to both operators and equipment. Some of the familiar names such as Air Europe, British Caledonian, Dan-Air and Pan Am have sadly disappeared, but these have been replaced by other ambitious carriers — some of which have also ceased trading in the meantime. Individual fleets change frequently due to the current trend of leasing aircraft for short periods, thereby increasing the risk of omissions and inaccuracies. Spain also produces its own problems due to a somewhat inconvenient habit nowadays of reregistering aircraft for little reason. As before, there has been no attempt to record companies in the process of setting up, because all too frequently they do not safely negotiate this first hurdle. The coverage is therefore similar to that of *abc Civil Aircraft Markings* but with more detail of operators' activities past and present.

Author's note: Incomplete registrations indicate aircraft on order.

First published 1986
Second edition 1996

ISBN 0 7110 2415 4

Published by Ian Allan Publishing

an imprint of Ian Allan Ltd, Terminal House, Station Approach, Shepperton, Surrey TW17 8AS. Printed by Ian Allan Printing Ltd, Coombelands House, Coombelands Lane, Addlestone, Surrey KT15 1HY.

Front cover: **Airbus A310-203.**
Aviation Picture Library

Back cover, top: **G-MONW – Airbus A320-2 12 of Monarch Airlines.**

Back cover, bottom: **LN-BRI – Boeing 737-405 of Braathens SAFE.**

Below: **G-AVMT – BAC One-Eleven 510ED of AB Shannon.**

Opposite: **G-UKLK – Airbus A320-212 of Leisure International Airways.**

All photographs by the author unless otherwise indicated.

CONTENTS

Opposite: EI-CKS – Boeing 737-2T5 of Ryanair.

Above: PH-KVI — Fokker 50 of KLMCity Hopper.

AB Shannon (7L)

United Kingdom

The airline was formed as a subsidiary of Air Bristol in late 1995 to operate scheduled services between Gatwick and Shannon. These started in December and are flown by a One-Eleven leased from European Air Charter.

FLEET:

BAC One-Eleven 510ED: G-AVMT

UK airport served: Gatwick.

Aer Lingus (EI/EIN)

PO Box 180, Dublin Airport, Co Dublin

Eire

Tel: (1) 705 22 22

Above: **EI-CLJ – BAe 146-300 of Aer Lingus**

Commercial operations began on 27 May 1936 when the Dragon EI-ABT operated a service between Dublin and Bristol/Whitchurch. By the end of the following year the network had grown to include routes from Dublin to the Isle of Man, Liverpool and London/Croydon. Although flying was suspended at the outbreak of the war, it was not long before Aer Lingus reintroduced the Liverpool schedule using both the DH86 Express and DC-3. Luckily the airline suffered no losses, despite its aircraft entering the Merseyside area where both attackers and defenders were much in evidence.

Aer Lingus restored the London route on 9 November 1945 using DC-3 EI-ACA for the inaugural run. Paris was added in the following June, joined at regular intervals by schedules to Amsterdam, Belfast, Brussels and Rome. By this time the fleet had increased in size with the arrival of some Vickers Vikings, but the type only remained a short time before being replaced with more DC-3s.

Nevertheless, the latter had to be replaced with something more modern sooner or later; the Viscount proving to be the choice. Friendships were employed for a time in the late 1950s/early 1960s, but these were replaced by four One-Elevens in 1965, which then remained with the Irish carrier until sold in Nigeria in 1991. Long-haul charters and schedules were maintained by Boeing 720s, 707s and 747s, but the use of a pair of 767s in the early 1990s was short-lived. Three Airbus A330s were ordered and delivered in 1994, whereupon the type began to take over the duties from the remaining 747s.

In the early 1980s, the airline's short-haul routes were transferred to Aer Lingus Commuter. Initially a Shorts 330 was used for a trial period, but with the venture proving a success, the carrier soon acquired four of the larger 360s. These in turn were replaced by four SAAB 340s in 1991, but in the meantime the fleet had increased in size with the arrival of the first of six Fokker 50s in 1989. Aer Lingus found it necessary to introduce jets to its main commuter routes in 1995, resulting in three BAe 146s being leased followed by a fourth in 1996.

FLEET:

Airbus A330-301: EI-CRK, EI-DUB, EI-JFK, EI-SHN

BAe146-300: EI-CLG, EI-CLH, EI-CLI, EI-CLJ

Boeing 737-448: EI-BXA, EI-BXB, EI-BXC, EI-BXD, EI-BXI, EI-BXK

Boeing 737-548: EI-CDA, EI-CDB, EI-CDC, EI-CDD, EI-CDE, EI-CDF, EI-CDG, EI-CDH, EI-CDS

Fokker F50: EI-FKA, EI-FKB, EI-FKC, EI-FKD, EI-FKE, EI-FKF

UK airports served: Birmingham, Bristol, East Midlands, Edinburgh, Glasgow, Heathrow, Jersey, Leeds/Bradford, Manchester Newcastle and Stansted.

Aer Turas (ATT)   Eire
Corballis Park, Dublin Airport   Tel: (1) 844 41 31

The carrier began operations in 1962 with a Rapide and a DC-3. Larger aircraft in the form of a Bristol Freighter and a DC-4 were introduced three years later allowing the airline to specialise in the movement of livestock. This activity has since continued but the types employed have been the Canadair CL-44 and DC-8, the latter comprising the current equipment. Transatlantic freight services are flown for Aer Lingus which is a major shareholder in Aer Turas.

FLEET:

Douglas DC-8-63AF: EI-BNA, EI-CGO

UK airports served: None regularly.

Aero Lloyd Flugreisen (YP/AEF)   Germany
Lessingstrasse 7–9, Postfach 2029,
D-6370 Oberusel   Tel: (6171) 641148

A fleet of three ex-Aviaco Caravelles was used by Aero Lloyd when the airline began operations in March 1981. These were soon replaced by a similar number of DC-9s which have themselves now given way to the more modern MD80 and A320/A321 types. Scheduled services were started on 31 October 1988, but this activity was ended in April 1992 leaving Aero Lloyd to concentrate on charter services from Berlin, Düsseldorf, Frankfurt and Hamburg.

Above: **D-ALLR —McD Douglas MD83 of Aero Lloyd.**

FLEET:

Airbus A320-232: D-ALAA, D-ALAB, D-ALAC	
Airbus A321-200: D-, D-, D-	
McD Douglas MD82: D-ALLS, D-ALLT	
McD Douglas MD83: D-AGWB, D-AGWC, D-ALLD, D-ALLE, D-ALLF, D-ALLK, D-ALLL, D-ALLM, D-ALLN, D-ALLO, D-ALLP, D-ALLQ, D-ALLR, D-ALLU, D-ALLV, D-ALLW	
McD Douglas MD87: D-ALLG, D-ALLJ	

UK airports served: None regularly, occasional charters only.

Aeroflot/Russia International (SU/AFL)   Russia
Leningradsky Prospekt 37, Moscow 125167   Tel: (095) 155 66 53

Although Aeroflot remains the largest airline in the world, there has been a considerable reduction in size during recent years with a multitude of smaller carriers emerging. Many of the latter's aircraft have been transferred from the main fleet, but continue to carry Aeroflot livery and, in many cases, titles.

FLEET:

Airbus A310-308: F-OGQQ, F-OGQR, F-OGQT, F-OGQU

Airbus A310-324: F-OGYM, F-OGYN, F-OGYP, F-OGYU, F-OGYV

Antonov An-124: RA-82005 to RA-82041

Boeing 767-3Y0ER: EI-CKD, EI-CKE, EI-, EI-

Douglas DC-10-30: N524MD

Ilyushin IL-62: RA-86450 to RA-86712

Ilyushin IL-76: RA-76350 to RA-76927

Ilyushin IL-86: RA-86002 to RA-86149

Ilyushin IL-96: RA-96001 to RA-96012

Tupolev Tu-134: RA-65020 to RA-65999

Tupolev Tu-154: RA-85001 to RA-85802

Also operated are Yak-40s, An-12s, An-22s and An-24s.

UK airports served: Gatwick, Heathrow, Manchester and Stansted.

Aerolineas Argentinas (AR/ARG)　　Argentina
Paseo Colon 185, 1063 Buenos Aires　　Tel: (1) 5341/5241

The carrier was formed in 1949 by an amalgamation of four companies, taking over the scheduled passenger and cargo operations in the process. Nowadays a large network of routes is flown to all parts of the Americas, Europe, New Zealand, South Africa and the Far East.

FLEET:

Boeing 747-287B: LV-MLO, LV-MLP, LV-MLR, LV-OEP, LV-OOZ, LV-OPA

Also operated are Airbus A310-324, Boeing 727/737 and McD Douglas MD88.

UK airport served: Heathrow.

Affretair (ZL/AFM)　　Zimbabwe
PO Box 655, Harare International Airport　　Tel: (4) 73 1781/9

Formed in 1965 as Air Trans Africa, the airline later became Zimbabwe's national freight carrier known as Affretair. Regular flights are operated to Amsterdam, Cairo, Dar es Salaam, Gatwick, Johannesburg, Kano, Lagos and Lilongwe. Charter work is also undertaken around Africa and the Middle East.

FLEET:

Douglas DC-8-55F: Z-WMJ, Z-WSB

UK airport served: Gatwick.

Left: RA-86560 — Ilyushin IL-62 of Aeroflot? Russia International.

African Airlines International (AIK)
Kenya
PO Box 74772, Nairobi

Tel: (2) 50 1319/50

Passenger and cargo charters are undertaken by this airline which was formed in 1987 with a pair of ex-Air Zimbabwe Boeing 707s.

FLEET:

Boeing 707-330B: 5Y-AXI, 5Y-AXM

Boeing 707-351B: 5Y-AXR, 5Y-BBI

UK airports served: None regularly.

African International Airways (AIN)
Swaziland
1 The Brunel Centre, Newton Road, Crawley, UK

Tel: (01293) 54 4706

This Swaziland-registered company was formed in 1985 to offer freight capacity to scheduled carriers when required.

FLEET:

Douglas DC-8-54F: 3D-ADV, 3D-AFR, 3D-AFX

UK airports served: None regularly.

African Safari Airways (QSC)
Kenya
Postfach 158, CH-4030 Basel Flughaven

Tel: (61) 325 29 41

Established in August 1967, the airline flies safari-style inclusive tours from Europe to African game-parks. For many years the airline employed a DC-8 for the work, but more recently an ex-KLM DC-10 has taken over the duties. When not in service the aircraft is normally based at Basel, Switzerland.

FLEET:

Douglas DC-10-30: PH-DTL

UK airport served: Gatwick.

Aigle Azur (ZI/AAF)
France
BP 24 Aéroport de Paris, F-95301
Cergy Pontoise Cédex

Tel: (1) 30 31 30 51

Formerly known as Lucas Aviation, the company was formed in 1977 as an air-taxi operator. It later became a regional airline flying both scheduled and charter services on routes which included links with Gatwick and northern France. These were ceased at the start of the 1996 summer programme.

Above: F-GGBV — SAAB SF340A of Aigle Azur.

FLEET:

Boeing 737-2K5: F-GMJD	
EMB-110P Bandeirante: F-GBGA	
SAAB SF340A: F-GGBV	

UK airports served: None regularly.

Air Afrique (RK/RKA) — Ivory Coast
BP 3927, 3 Avenue Joseph Anoma, Abidjan 01   Tel: 20 30 00

Created in March 1961 by a consortium of a number of West African states with strong French ties, naturally regular links with France have always been maintained. Nowadays many of the major European cities are included in the airline's network of scheduled services, together with African, North American and Far Eastern destinations.

FLEET:

Airbus A300B4-203: TU-TAO, TU-TAS, TU-TAT	
Airbus A300-605R: TU-TAH, TU-TAI	
Airbus A310-304: TU-TAC, TU-TAD, TU-TAE, TU-TAF, TU-TAU	

UK airport served: Gatwick.

Air Alfa (H7/LFA) — Turkey
Yesilkoy Halkali Asfalti 9, A-Blok, Kat.2, TR-34810 Florya-Istanbul   Tel: (212) 663 8287

One of a number of airlines created in Turkey as a result of the country's growing appeal for leisure travellers, Air Alfa was established in 1992 for European IT work with Boeing 727s. Subsequently it acquired larger equipment to cope with the demand for capacity.

FLEET:

Airbus A300B4: TC-ALG, TC-ALN, TC-ALR, TC-ALS

Boeing 727-230: TC-ALK, TC-ALM

UK airports served: East Midlands, Gatwick, Heathrow.

Air Algérie (AH/DAH)   Algeria
1 Place Maurice-Audin, Algiers   Tel: (2) 64 24 28

As the African colonies of the major powers were granted independence, so a number of fledgling airlines emerged, however fragile the economy. In Algeria the Compagnie Générale de Transports Aériens (CGTA) was formed in 1946 as a non-scheduled carrier. Gradually, regular services were introduced, particularly on the traditional Algiers to Paris, Marseille and Toulouse routes. A merger with the Compagnie Air Transport in April 1953 further established the airline which then adopted the name Air Algérie. Both international and domestic route networks expanded, but it was the delivery of the company's first jet type — a Caravelle — in 1960 that enabled direct links to be offered to Paris. This, in turn, no doubt influenced the decision to designate the airline as the nation's flag carrier three years later, before eventually becoming wholly owned by the government in 1972. Scheduled services are now flown to numerous points in Europe and the Middle East.

FLEET:

Airbus A310-203: 7T-VJC, 7T-VJD, 7T-VJE, 7T-VJF

Boeing 727-2D6: 7T-VEA, 7T-VEB, 7T-VEH, 7T-VEI, 7T-VEM, 7T-VEP, 7T-VET, 7T-VEU, 7T-VEV, 7T-VEW, 7T-VEX

Boeing 737-2D6C: 7T-VED, 7T-VES

Boeing 737-2D6: 7T-VEF, 7T-VEG, 7T-VEJ, 7T-VEK, 7T-VEL, 7T-VEN, 7T-VEO, 7T-VEQ, 7T-VER, 7T-VEY

Boeing 737-2T4: 7T-VEZ, 7T-VJA, 7T-VJB

Boeing 767-3D6: 7T-VJG, 7T-VJH, 7T-VJI

Also operated are two Hercules and eight Friendships.

UK airports served: Gatwick and Heathrow.

Air Atlanta Iceland (CC/ABD)   Iceland
Atlanta House, PO Box 80, 270 Mosfellsbaer   Tel: (1) 66 77 00

Formed in 1986, the airline specialises in the operation of scheduled passenger and cargo services on behalf of carriers in need of additional capacity. It began operating IT charters in its own right in May 1993 by flying travellers to destinations in Germany, Ireland, Italy and Spain. The fleet employed varies considerably in size according to the demand.

FLEET:

Boeing 737-230C: TF-ABF, TF-ABX	
Boeing 737-266: TF-ABG	
Boeing 747-1D1: TF-ABO, TF-ABS	
Boeing 747-133: TF-ABR	
Boeing 747-246B: TF-ABI	
L1011-385 TriStar 1: TF-ABE, TF-ABH, TF-ABM	

UK airports served: None regularly.

Air Atlantique (DG/AAG)   United Kingdom
Hangar 5, Coventry Airport   Tel: (01203) 307566

The airline started as an air-taxi operator with its headquarters in Jersey, but in 1977 charter work began using DC-3s. The number operated has grown over the years and the airline now finds employment on oil spill duties or cargo charters. Pleasure flights are also offered throughout the summer season, always proving a popular feature at air shows. In addition to the DC-3 freighters, Air Atlantique also operates three Electras and two DC-6s, the extra capacity being useful for some of the regular contract work undertaken. The company has become involved in scheduled passenger services on at least two occasions, the first being in 1988 when it began flying on the Southampton–Channel Islands routes with an elderly HS748. This enterprise was soon dropped, but in the early 1990s there was another attempt made — this time operating as Air Corbière with a Metro and a Caravan — to link the Channel Islands with such airports as Gloucester and Coventry, but once again the services were suspended. The company now trades as Atlantic Airways, Atlantic Cargo and Atlantic Reconnaissance.

FLEET:

Atlantic Reconnaissance:	
Cessna 404: G-EXEX, G-TASK	
BN-2A Islander: G-BCEN	
Douglas C-47: G-AMCA, G-AMHJ, G-AMPO, G-AMPY, G-AMSV, G-AMYJ, G-ANAF	
Atlantic Airways:	
Cessna 404: G-MIND	
Douglas C-47: G-AMPZ	
PA-31-350 Navajo Chieftain: G-NERC	
SA227AC Metro: G-BUKA	
Atlantic Cargo:	
Douglas C-47: G-AMRA	
Douglas DC-6A: G-APSA, G-SIXC	
L188CF Electra: G-LOFA, G-LOFB, G-LOFC	

UK airports served: *Ad hoc* freight charters and pleasure flying take the aircraft to many locations, with the main base at Coventry.

Air Baltic (BT/BTI)   Latvia
Riga Airport, Riga LV-1053, Latvia   Tel: (7) 20 70 69

In 1995 the Latvian Government decided that a new airline should be created to become the national carrier. As a result Air Baltic took over the scheduled routes previously flown by Latavio and Baltic International.

FLEET:

Avro RJ70: YL-BAK, YL-BAL, YL-BAN

SAAB SF340A: YL-BAG

UK airport served: Gatwick.

Air Belfast (7L)   United Kingdom
PO Box 92, Patchway, Bristol   Tel: (0117) 936 4932

The airline was created as a direct result of the peace initiative in Northern Ireland. As a part of the Air Bristol Group, Air Belfast started scheduled flights between Belfast International and Stansted on 1 March 1995. Two One-Elevens were leased from European Air Charter for the high frequency sorties, but these ended after one year.

FLEET:

Leased as required

UK airports served: None regularly.

Air Belgium (AJ/ABB)   Belgium
Vilvoordelaan 192, B-1930 Zaventem   Tel: (2) 720 61 20

When the carrier was launched in May 1979 it was known as Abelag Airways, but during the following year the present name was adopted. Charter flights are operated to most of the south European holiday destinations, together with transatlantic ITs from Brussels.

FLEET:

Boeing 737-3Q8: OO-ILK

Boeing 737-46B: OO-ILJ

UK airports served: None regularly.

Air Berlin (AB/BER)   Germany
Flughafen Tegel, W-1000 Berlin 51   Tel: (30) 410 12781

The airline was formed in 1978 and has subsequently operated IT flights on behalf of German tour operators. This activity takes the carrier's aircraft to many of the Mediterranean airports together with some in North Africa and the Canaries.

Above: **D-ABAE — Boeing 737-46J of Air Berlin.**

FLEET:

Boeing 737-4K5: D-ABAB	
Boeing 737-4Y0: D-ABAD, D-ABAF	
Boeing 737-46J: D-ABAE, D-ABAG, D-ABAH, D-ABAI, D-ABAK, D-ABAL	

UK airports served: None regularly.

Air Bristol (AZX) — United Kingdom
PO Box 92, Patchway, Bristol   Tel: (0117) 936 4932

When Air Bristol was formed in February 1993 it was intended that it would create a network of regional scheduled services from a hub at Bristol/Filton. Any development of the site into a commercial airport requires planning approval from the local authority and depends on the results of a public inquiry. In the meantime, Air Bristol has concentrated on *ad hoc* charter flights and the regular links between Filton and the Airbus plant at Toulouse. Air Bristol's livery is the same as that of Air Belfast with the exception of the titles carried on the aircraft.

Below: **G-AVMW — BAC One-Eleven 510ED of Air Bristol.**

FLEET:
BAC One-Eleven 510ED: G-AVMW

UK airports served: Bristol/Filton and Stansted; others irregularly.

Air Canada (AC/ACA)　　　　　Canada
PO Box 14000, Montreal, Quebec　　　　Tel: (514) 422 5000

Above: **C-GAGA — Boeing 747-233B of Air Canada.**

During the 1930s there were numerous small airlines in Canada, many of them gradually amalgamating under the ownership of Canadian Pacific Railways. In 1937 there was a proposal that the airline should enter an association with the government to form Trans Canada Airlines, but this was rejected. Subsequently, the railway company went on to create Canadian Pacific Airlines in 1942. Undeterred by the setback, the government launched TCA anyway, with passenger services starting in 1939. Two years later the company introduced its first major international schedule when New York was added to the coverage. Regular transatlantic flights began in 1943 on behalf of the government and were of the utmost importance to the war effort. This operational experience was of great benefit to TCA when it was able to commence commercial services over the same route in May 1947.

During the 1960s the fleet was upgraded with jet equipment when DC-8s were received, the basic type that served the airline until the advent of the Boeing 747 and TriStar. However, by the time that these wide-bodied machines were in use, the government had changed the name of the flag carrier to Air Canada which in 1964 was considered to express the country's bilingual make-up more effectively and also to reflect the airline's growing overseas presence. It began using the twin-engine Boeing 767 for transatlantic crossings in 1985, a development which was still quite rare although not unique. The company became fully privatised in July 1989.

FLEET:

Airbus A340-313: C-FTNP, C-FTNQ (plus six on order)

Boeing 747-133: C-FTOC, C-FTOD, C-FTOE

Boeing 747-233B: C-GAGA, C-GAGB, C-GAGC

Boeing 747-433: C-GAGL, C-GAGM, C-GAGN

Boeing 767-209ER: C-FUCL, C-FUCM, C-FVNM

Boeing 767-233ER: C-FBEF, C-FBEG, C-FBEM, C-GAVC, C-GAVF, C-GDSP, C-GDSS, C-GDSU, C-GDSY

Boeing 767-333ER: C-FMWP, C-FMWQ, C-FMWU, C-FMWV, C-FMWY, C-FMXC

Also operated are DC-9s, Canadair Regional Jets, Airbus A320-211s and Boeing 767-233s which are not of the extended range variety.

UK airports served: Glasgow, Heathrow and Manchester.

Air Charter (SF/ACF) — France
4 rue de la Couture, Silic 318,
F-94588 Rengis Cédex
Tel: (1) 45 60 33 00

The company was formed by Air France in February 1966 as a wholly-owned subsidiary specifically for the operation of charters and ITs. Later, Air Inter received a 20% shareholding in exchange for an undertaking that it would not indulge in any non-scheduled services at the expense of Air Charter. The carrier's aircraft are occasionally used by Air France when short of capacity, but most of the activity involves flights to the holiday areas of the Mediterranean. Some aircraft are operated jointly with Euralair or on behalf of other carriers.

FLEET:

Airbus A300B4-203: F-BVGI, F-BVGT

Airbus A320-211: F-GFKX

Airbus A320-212: F-GLGM, F-GLGN

Boeing 737-2K5: F-GFLV, F-GFLX

Boeing 737-53A: F-GHXM

UK airports served: Edinburgh, Newcastle and Stansted.

Air China (CA/CCA) — China
Capital International Airport, 100621 Beijing
Tel: (1) 456 32 20

Prior to 1988 the airline operated the international services of the Civil Aviation Administration of China (CAAC), but it was renamed in that year following a government directive. This split the CAAC into separate airlines, each with its own identity to operate domestic, regional and international schedules. Air China flies to a number of destinations in Europe including a link between London and Beijing.

FLEET:

Boeing 747-2J6B: B-2446, B-2448, B-2450

Boeing 747-2J6F: B-2462

Boeing 747SP-J6: B-2438, B-2442, B-2452

Boeing 747SP-27: B-2454

Boeing 747-4J6: B-2443, B-2445, B-2447, B-2464, B-2466

Boeing 747-4J6 (SCD): B-2456, B-2458, B-2460

UK airport served: Heathrow.

Air Club International (HB/CLI)　　Canada
11905 Cargo Road, Mirabel, Quebec　　Tel: (514) 476 35 55

The company was formed in May 1993, but charter flights only began in June 1994. Services are offered from main Canadian cities to a number of European destinations together with others to Florida, Hawaii and the Caribbean.

FLEET:

Airbus A310-324: C-GCIL, C-GCIO, C-GCIT, C-GCIV

Boeing 747-128: C-GCIS

UK airports served: Belfast, Cardiff, Gatwick, Glasgow and Manchester.

Air Engiadina (RQ/RQX)　　Switzerland
PO Box 1377, General Aviation Centre,
CH-8058 Zürich　　Tel: (1) 814 14 40

Scheduled services are flown by the airline which was formed in 1987. These radiate from both Zürich and Bern to points in Austria, Germany, The Netherlands and the UK. Stansted was the UK gateway for the first year of operation, but in March 1995 the airline moved to London City, which is now linked thrice-daily with the Swiss capital by a Dornier 328.

FLEET:

BAe Jetstream 31: HB-AEA

Dornier Do328-100: HB-AEE, HB-AEF, HB-AEG, HB-AEH, HB-AEI

UK airport served: London City.

Air Europa (UX/AEA)   Spain
Gran Via Asima 23, Poligono Son Castello,
E-07009 Palma   **Tel: (71) 17 81 00**

Operations began in 1986, two years after being formed as a member of the Airlines of Europe Group. The airline survived the collapse of the latter organisation in 1991 by Spanish interests taking over the financial stake held by the UK company. Air Europa (the trading name of Air Espana) has continued to specialise in IT charters from Northern and Western Europe to mainland Spain, together with the Balearic and Canary Islands. Long-haul flights are also undertaken to the Far East, Cuba and the Caribbean area.

FLEET:

Boeing 737-3Y0: EC-FJZ, EC-FKJ, EC-FVJ, EC-GEQ, EC-GFU
Boeing 737-375: EC-FKI, EC-GEU
Boeing 737-3M8: EC-GGD, EC-GHD
Boeing 737-3Q8: EC-FUT, EC-FXC, EC-FYF
Boeing 737-4Q8: EC-FXP, EC-FXQ
Boeing 737-4Y0: EC-FZZ EC-GAZ, EC-GBN
Boeing 757-236: EC-FEE, EC-FEF, EC-FFK, EC-FTL, EC-GBX, EC-GCA, EC-GCB
Boeing 767-204: EC-

UK airports served: Various for IT charter flights.

Left: **HB-AEF — Dornier Do328-100 of Air Engiadina.** *A. S. Wright*

Above: **EC-FXP — Boeing 737-4Q8 of Air Europa**

Air Europe Italy (PE/AEL)   Italy
Corso Sempione 15A, I-21013 Gallarate   Tel: (331) 77 21 11

This element of the former Airlines of Europe Group was created in 1989 using aircraft transferred from the UK company. When the latter collapsed in March 1991, the Italian airline managed to survive and now operates its aircraft on IT charter work.

FLEET:

Boeing 767-330ER: EI-CIY, EI-
Boeing 767-35HER: EI-CJA, EI-CJB
Boeing 767-3Q8ER: EI-CMQ
Boeing 767-352ER: EI-CLS

UK airports served: None regularly.

Air Exel Commuter (XT/AXL)   Netherlands
PO Box 300, Vliegveldweg 17, 6236 ZN Maastricht   Tel: (43) 65 07 00

At one time there were a number of commuter airlines within the Air Exel Group, all hopeful of providing a comprehensive route network of regional services in Europe. In the event few started operations, with only Air Exel Commuter still active, providing services from Maastricht.

FLEET:

EMB-120RT Brasilia: PH-XLA, PH-XLB

UK airport served: Stansted.

Air Foyle (GS/UPA)   United Kingdom
Halcyon House, Percival Way, Luton, Bedfordshire   Tel: (01582) 419792

The company was formed in May 1978 as an air-taxi operator, but since then it has moved into other fields of activity. Freight services have been flown for TNT for some years, the BAe 146s visiting various European airports during the course of their nocturnal activities. In 1993 the company was responsible for the flights needed for the IT programme marketed by Sunseeker Leisure, a BA Boeing 737-300 being leased to cover the duties. In 1994 Air Foyle operated a pair of Airbus A320s for Airworld, a new airline formed to provide IT charters. With the demise of Ambassador Airways at the end of the year, some of its commitments were taken over by the Luton-based company, together with two Boeing 737-200s. These joined Sabre Airways, an airline set up by Air Foyle for charter work. In December 1993 the latter won a contract to provide standby aircraft for oil spills, whereupon a Hercules and an IL-76 were acquired for this purpose. The company is also able to handle outsize freight loads by using one of a number of An-124 Ruslans to which it has access.

FLEET:

An-124 Ruslan: UR-82007, UR-82008, UR-82009, UR-82027, UR-82029

Ilyushin IL-76MD: UR-78755 (operated for oil spill response)

L.100-30 Hercules: N901SJ (operated for oil spill response)

UK airports served: Belfast, Birmingham, Edinburgh, Luton and Stansted.

Air France (AF/AFR) — France
1 Square Max Hymans, F-75757 Paris 15   Tel: (1) 43 23 81 81

The French national airline was created on 30 August 1933 following the amalgamation of an assortment of small carriers. Routes to most of Europe's major cities were included in the network with the exception of Madrid, Stockholm and Rome. The company developed the Paris–London link, with some priority given to the provision of a high standard of comfort, wherever possible in aircraft capable of superior performances to those of the competitors. By the outbreak of World War 2, Air France was, in company with Deutsche Luft Hansa, one of the world's leading airlines, but this situation changed after 1939.

In February 1941 the carrier was renamed Réseau Aérien Français, at the same time incorporating three smaller operators. On 20 December the name Air France ceased to exist, an event which paved the way for the German flag carrier to take over the French company's possessions, both human and material. None the less, a token operation was mounted in North Africa by a few escapees which helped in the task of getting the airline fully established again in 1945. Postwar, Air France was formally reactivated on 1 January 1946, but large orders for aircraft had already been placed in advance. The traditional Paris–London link was restored on 11 October 1945 by the temporary wartime organisation, so the national carrier got off to a good start. By 1952 Air France was the largest airline in the world in terms of route mileage.

Always keen to remain in the forefront, the company introduced Comet 1s on its Paris–Rome–Beirut schedules in 1953, while Viscounts took over the London operation. Unfortunately, circumstances forced the cessation of the jet services, but not before the airline had announced its intention to employ the Comet on its prestige short-haul sectors. In 1959 a second start was made, but this time it was the Caravelle that launched a long and successful partnership with Air France.

Supersonic services began with Concorde in January 1976 and have continued to the present day, albeit only on the Paris–New York run in recent years. The airline has always been a loyal supporter of Airbus products, playing a major role in the early success of the A300.

FLEET:

Airbus A300B2-101: F-BVGA, F-BVGB, F-BVGC

Airbus A300B4-203: F-BVGG, F-BVGH, F-BVGJ, F-BVGL, F-BVGM, F-BVGN, F-BVGO

Airbus A310-203: F-GEMA, F-GEMB, F-GEMC, F-GEMD, F-GEME, F-GEMG

Airbus A310-304: F-GEMN, F-GEMO, F-GEMP, F-GEMQ

Airbus A320-111: F-GFKA, F-GFKB, F-GFKD, F-GFKE, F-GFKF, F-GFKG

Airbus A320-211: F-GFKH, F-GFKI, F-GFKJ, F-GFKK, F-GFKL, F-GFKM, F-GFKN, F-GFKO, F-GFKP, F-GFKQ, F-GFKR, F-GFKS, F-GFKT, F-GFKU, F-GFKV, F-GFKY, F-GFKZ

Airbus A340-211: F-GLZD, F-GLZE, F-GLZF, F-GLZK

Airbus A340-311: F-GLZA, F-GLZB, F-GLZC, F-GLZG, F-GLZH, F-GLZI, F-GLZJ, F-GLZL, F-GLZM, F-GLZN

Boeing 737-228: F-GBYA, F-GBYB, F-GBYC, F-GBYD, F-GBYE, F-GBYF, F-GBYG, F-GBYH, F-GBYI, F-GBYJ, F-GBYK, F-GBYL, F-GBYM, F-GBYN, F-GBYO, F-GBYP, F-GBYQ

Boeing 737-33A: F-GFUA, F-GFUD, F-GFUJ, F-GHVM, F-GHVN, F-GHVO

Boeing 737-528: F-GJNA, F-GJNB, F-GJNC, F-GJND, F-GJNE, F-GJNF, F-GJNG, F-GJNH, F-GJNI, F-GJNJ, F-GJNK, F-GJNM, F-GJNN, F-GJNO

Boeing 747-128: F-BPVF, F-BPVJ, F-BPVL, F-BPVM, F-BPVP

Boeing 747-228B: F-BPVS, F-BPVT, F-BPVU, F-BPVX, F-BPVY, F-GCBA, F-GCBB, F-GCBD, F-GCBF, F-GCBI, F-GCBJ

Boeing 747-228F: F-BPVR, F-BPVV, F-BPVZ, F-GCBE, F-GCBG, F-GCBH, F-GCBK, F-GCBL, F-GCBM

Boeing 747-2B3B: F-BTDG, F-BTDH

Boeing 747-2B3F: F-GBOX, F-GPAN

Boeing 747-3B3: F-GETA, F-GETB

Boeing 747-4B3: F-GEXA, F-GEXB

Boeing 747-428: F-GISA, F-GISB, F-GISC, F-GISD, F-GISE, F-GITA, F-GITB, F-GITC, F-GITD, F-GITE, F-GITF, F-GITH

Boeing 767-27EER: F-GHGD, F-GHGE (both operated by Balkan)

Boeing 767-3Q8ER: F-GHGF, F-GHGG

Boeing 767-37EER: F-GHGH

Boeing 767-328ER: F-GHGI, F-GHGJ

Concorde 101: F-BTSC, F-BTSD, F-BVFA, F-BVFB, F-BVFC, F-BVFF

F27 Friendship Mk 500: F-BPUA, F-BPUC, F-BPUD, F-BPUE, F-BPUF, F-BPUG, F-BPUH, F-BPUJ, F-BSUN, F-BSUO

UK airports served: Birmingham, Edinburgh, Glasgow, Heathrow, Manchester and Stansted.

Air Holland Charter (GG/AHR) Netherlands
PO Box 75116, NL-1117 ZR Schiphol Oost Tel: (20) 658 44 44

The airline was known as Air Holland when operations began in August 1988, but after some reorganisation, the present name was adopted in November 1991. At the same time the fleet was reduced in size, but the carrier continued to operate IT charters from Holland to the Mediterranean area and the Canary Islands.

Above: PH-OZB — Boeing 737-3YO of Air Holland.

FLEET:

Boeing 737-33A: PH-	
Boeing 737-3L9: PH-OZA	
Boeing 737-3Y0: PH-OZB	
Boeing 757-27B: PH-AHE, PH-AHI	
Boeing 757-2T7: G-MONC	

UK airports served: None regularly.

Air Hong Kong (LD/AHK) — Hong Kong

Block 2, Tien Chu Centre, 1E Mok Cheong Street, Kowloon

Tel: 761 85 88

The airline was formed in November 1986 to operate cargo services, an activity which began in February 1988 on a charter basis. Approval was received to start scheduled flights to a large number of destinations worldwide, with the first batch introduced in October 1989. In early 1994 Cathay Pacific acquired a 75% share in the company, although Air Hong Kong has continued to operate as an independent carrier.

FLEET:

Boeing 747-249F: VR-HKO	
Boeing 747-2L5B: VR-HMD, VR-HME, VR-HMF	

UK airport served: Manchester.

Air India (AI/AIC) — India

Air India Building, Nariman Point, Bombay 400 021

Tel: (22) 202 41 42

From 1932 until 1946 Tata Airlines was largely responsible for India's air transport system, flying mainly mail services around the country with Rapides. At the outbreak of war the aircraft came under military control when all commercial activities were suspended for the duration. A new start was made in 1946 with the creation of Air India, although after the country's independence 'International' was added to the title. The first long-haul service was inaugurated shortly after the arrival of the Constellations, this type thereafter maintaining the Bombay–London route. It was not long before other European cities were added to the network, these including Rome, Paris and Düsseldorf.

It was an era when nationalisation was fashionable around the world, with India being no exception. Consequently, in 1953 all domestic services came under the control of Indian Airlines, with Air India International assuming responsibility for all others. It brought some fairly rapid expansion which was covered by the acquisition of some Super Constellations, initially for use on the London run. During February and March 1960 the airline took delivery of three Boeing 707s, giving the company the opportunity to extend the UK route across the Atlantic to New York. As more of the type were delivered, so the piston-engined machines were sold, leaving the 707s to become the mainstay of the fleet until 1971 when the first 747 was taken on strength. Airbus A300s took over the schedules to the Gulf States in 1977, with the longer range A310 selected for routes uneconomic for 747 operations.

Above: **VT-EBE — Boeing 747-237B of Air India.** *A. S. Wright*

FLEET:

Airbus A310-304:	VT-EJG, VT-EJH, VT-EJI, VT-EJJ, VT-EJK, VT-EJL, VT-EQS, VT-EQT
Airbus A310-324:	C-GCIL, C-GCIO, V2-LEC, V2-LED
Boeing 747-212B:	VT-ENQ
Boeing 747-237B:	VT-EBE, VT-EBN, VT-EDU, VT-EFJ, VT-EFU, VT-EGA, VT-EGB, VT-EGC
Boeing 747-337:	VT-EPW, VT-EPX
Boeing 747-437:	VT-ESM, VT-ESN, VT-ESO, VT-ESP, VT-EVA, VT-EVB, VT-
L1011-385 TriStar 500:	V2-LEJ, V2-LEK, V2-LEO

UK airports served: Birmingham, Heathrow.

Air Inter is the main French domestic airline, which was set up in November 1954 to provide passenger and charter services. In 1977 an agreement was reached with Air France that the latter activity would cease in return for a 20% stake in Air Charter, a subsidiary of the flag carrier. Since January 1990 Air Inter has also been a member of the Air France Group, the parent holding 70% of the company. Air Inter has remained independent and is now allowed to operate to any destination. When Air France completes its proposed restructuring exercise in 1997, it is likely that there will be one airline created from the various members of the Group.

FLEET:

Airbus A300B2: F-BUAF, F-BUAH, F-BUAI, F-BUAJ, F-BUAK, F-BUAN, F-BUAO, F-BUAP, F-GBEA	
Airbus A300B4: F-BUAL, F-BUAQ	
Airbus A319-100: F-GPMA, F-GPMB, F-GPMC, F-GPMD, F-GPME, F-GPMF, F-GPMG, F-GPMH, F-GPMI	
Airbus A320-111: F-GGEA, F-GGEB, F-GGEC, F-GGEE, F-GGEF, F-GGEG	
Airbus A320-211: F-GHQA, F-GHQB, F-GHQC, F-GHQD, F-GHQE, F-GHQF, F-GHQG, F-GHQH, F-GHQI, F-GHQJ, F-GHQK, F-GHQL, F-GHQM, F-GHQO, F-GHQP, F-GHQQ, F-GHQR, F-GJVA, F-GJVB, F-GJVC, F-GJVD, F-GJVE, F-GJVF, F-GJVG, F-GJVV, F-GJVW, F-GJVX, F-GJVY, F-GJVZ	
Airbus A321-111: F-GMZA, F-GMZB, F-GMZC, F-GMZD, F-GMZE, F-GMZF, F-GMZG	
Airbus A330-301: F-GMDA, F-GMDB, F-GMDC, F-GMDD,	
Fokker 100: F-GPXA, F-GPXB, F-GPXC, F-GPXD, F-GPXE	

UK airports served: Heathrow.

The airline was formed in May 1980 and now operates scheduled and charter services from its Paris base to Avignon, Strasbourg and Toulouse using BAe 146s. The latter are also used for the night mail run between CDG and Avignon and also for the regular service between CDG and London City which was launched in 1995.

FLEET:

BAe 146-200QC: F-GLNI, F-GMMP, F-GOMA

UK airports served: Gatwick, London City, Manchester and Stansted.

Air Kilroe (9R/AKL)   United Kingdom
Hangar 6, Manchester International Airport   Tel: (0161) 436 2055

Air-taxi services from Manchester have been operated by the company since
1978. These have included regular runs to Teesside on behalf of ICI. Scheduled
services were added in September 1993 to link its base with Cardiff twice on
weekdays in association with Business Air, but the operation was ended in late
1995.

FLEET:
BAe Jetstream 31: G-OAKI, G-OAKJ, G-OAKA

UK airports served: Manchester and Teesside.

Air Lanka (UL/ALK)   Sri Lanka
37 York Street, Colombo 1   Tel: (1) 73 55 55

Scheduled passenger and charter operations began on 1 September 1979, some
eight months after the company was founded. Actually it was continuing the
activities of Air Ceylon as the national carrier, but obviously a name change was
necessary to reflect the identity of the newly-established Sri Lanka. Its
predecessor had been formed in 1947 to operate three DC-3s for services
between the island and India. After securing an agreement with Australian
National Airways in 1949 involving services to London and Sydney, two DC-4s
were purchased. KLM took over the Australian carrier's financial interests in
1956, one of the consequences being that a new route was opened to
Amsterdam. All international operations ceased in 1961, but a London link was
reintroduced in the following year in association with BOAC. Since the change
to Air Lanka a considerable number of international services have been
launched to European airports, the Gulf States and the Far East.

FLEET:
Airbus A340-311: 4R-ADA, 4R-ADB, 4R-ADC
L1011-385 TriStar 50: 4R-ULE
L1011-385 TriStar 100: 4R-ULC
L1011-385 TriStar 500: 4R-ULA, 4R-ULB
Also operated Airbus A320s.

UK airport served: Heathrow.

Air Liberté (VD/LIB)   France
1 Rue du Courson, Senia 128 Thais,
F-94517 Rungis Cédex   Tel: (1) 46 86 25 00

The airline began operations in 1988 with charter flights from French airports
to various destinations around the Mediterranean and Canary Islands. Air
Liberté later moved into the scheduled scene when it received approval to fly
on routes in competition with Air Inter and Air France, with the result that the

airline began linking Gatwick with Paris/Orly four times per day with MD83s. It also flies on domestic sectors with the same equipment. An agreement was reached with Euralair in late 1995 whereby Air Liberté took over the latter's scheduled services. A transatlantic link was launched in April 1996 using a leased A310.The airline is likely to be taken over by AOM or BA due to financial problems.

FLEET:

Airbus A300-622R: F-GHEF, F-GHEG	
Airbus A310-221: F-GOCJ, F-GPDJ	
Airbus A310-324: F-GHEJ	
Boeing 737-21OC: F-GJDL	
Boeing 737-222: F-GCJL, F-GCLL, F-GCSL	
Boeing 747-121: F-GIMJ	
Douglas DC-10-30: F-GPVA, F-GPVB, F-GPVD, F-GPVE	
McD Douglas MD83: F-GFZB, F-GHEB, F-GHEC, F-GHED, F-GHEI, F-GHEK, F-GHHO, F-GHHP	

UK airport served: Gatwick

Air Littoral (FU/LIT) — France
417 Rue Samuel Morse, F-34961 Montpellier — Tel: (67) 20 67 20

Above: **F-GIGO — Aérospatiale ATR72-201 of Air Littoral.**

The airline was established at Montpellier in 1972 to undertake scheduled services in southern France. Islanders were used at first, but expansion of the network in 1978 brought the first Bandeirante into the fleet. Air Littoral became an international carrier in June 1980 when operations began on the Montpellier–Perpignan–Valencia route which was flown thrice weekly. More Bandeirantes were taken on strength as the number of schedules increased, eventually leading to the addition of larger equipment. In 1988 the airline merged with Compagnie Aérienne du Languedoc, while in 1990 Fokker 100s were introduced on to the regional services flown on behalf of Air France and Air Inter.

FLEET:

Aérospatiale ATR42-310: F-GEGD, F-GEGE, F-GEGF, F-GFYN

Aérospatiale ATR42-512: F-GPYA, F-GPYB, F-GPYC, F-GPYD, F-GPYE, F-GPYF

Aérospatiale ATR72-201: F-GIGO

Canadair Regional Jet 100ER: F-GLIJ, F-GLIK, F-GLIY, F-GLIZ, F-GNME, F-GNMN, F-GPYP

EMB-120RT Brasilia: F-GFEO, F-GFEP, F-GFEQ, F-GFER, F-GFIN, F-GHIA, F-GHIB, F-GJAK

Fokker 70: F-GLIS, F-GLIT, F-GLIU, F-GLIV, F-GLIX

Fokker 100: F-GLIR

UK airports served: Gatwick, Manchester and Stansted.

Air Malta (KM/AMC)   Malta
Luqa, Malta GC   Tel: 82 43 30

The newly-formed, government-controlled, Air Malta began operations on 1 April 1974 with two Boeing 720s leased from Pakistan International. Scheduled services were introduced to Birmingham, Frankfurt, London, Manchester, Paris, Rome and Tripoli although some were only weekly trips. Traffic steadily increased until, by the end of the 1970s, five 720s were in use. A two-year lease was taken on three Transavia 737s during the early 1980s, enabling the new and more efficient type to take over the bulk of the operations from the thirsty 720s, which were reserved for peak periods only. The carrier's satisfaction with the twinjet prompted an order for three with deliveries specified for 1983, at which point the leased specimens were returned to their owner. The first of another three examples of the Series 200 variant arrived in 1987, while in 1990 an Airbus A320 joined the fleet. Nevertheless, Air Malta was still frequently short of capacity and often leased in a Boeing 727 for the summer seasons, but a more permanent solution was

Below: 9H-ABF — Boeing 737-2Y5 of Air Malta.

found by adding a second A320 and three 737-300s in 1993. None of its jet types were particularly suitable for the airline's short regional services, so an ATP was leased from SATA Air Azores while various types were evaluated. Eventually it was announced that the Avro RJ70 had been chosen, four of which joined Air Malta in 1994/95, releasing the three original 737-200s in the process. During the same year, the airline employed an A310 leased from Lufthansa for its busier routes such as London. The same type was similarly employed in 1995, but this time it was an ex-Kuwait machine obtained via the manufacturer for one year. For the 1996 season an A320 was leased from Adria and a 737-200 from Air New Zealand. Malta Air Charter, a subsidiary company of the national carrier, operates a regular link with neighbouring Gozo using a pair of Mil Mi-8P helicopters.

FLEET:

Airbus A320-211: 9H-ABP, 9H-ABQ	
Avro RJ70: 9H-ACM, 9H-ACN, 9H-ACO, 9H-ACP	
Boeing 737-2Y5: 9H-ABE, 9H-ABF	
Boeing 737-3Y5: 9H-ABR, 9H-ABS, 9H-ABT	

UK airports served: Belfast, Birmingham, Bristol, Cardiff, East Midlands, Edinburgh, Exeter, Gatwick, Glasgow, Heathrow, Humberside, Leeds/Bradford, Liverpool, Manchester, Newcastle and Stansted.

Air Mauritius (MK/MAU) — Mauritius

PO Box 441, 5 President John Kennedy Street, Port Louis — Tel: (208) 77 00

During the first five years following its creation in June 1967, Air Mauritius acted mainly as a handling agent for other carriers. Flight operations started in a small way in 1972, gradually expanding to include inter-island and, later, international services. A Boeing 707 was leased from British Airways until 1981, whereupon the source of its equipment changed to South African Airways. A need to offer a more modern type prompted the two-year lease of a 747SP in 1984, principally for use on the long-haul European sectors. It was during this period that Air Mauritius began to evaluate wide-bodied twins for its future fleet, eventually selecting the Boeing 767. In addition, the airline opted for the Airbus A340, three of which were ordered with deliveries spread over several years. In the meantime, two of the type were leased in 1994 for service entry in the spring.

FLEET:

Airbus A340-312: 3B-NAT, 3B-NAU, 3B-NAV, 3B-NAY, 3B-	
Boeing 767-23BER: 3B-NAK, 3B-NAL	
Boeing 767-328ER: 3B-NAZ	
Also operated are ATR42s.	

UK airports served: Heathrow and Manchester.

The carrier was known as Tasman Empire Airways when it was formed in 1939 to provide a link between Australia and New Zealand. The two countries, together with Britain, were involved in the enterprise which commenced operations in April 1940 when an Empire flying boat completed the first trip. The British interests were acquired by Australia in 1953, but in 1961 the airline became wholly owned by its homeland. On 1 April 1965 TEAL changed its identity to become Air New Zealand, a name which was retained after a merger with New Zealand National Airways Corporation in April 1978. The latter had previously been responsible for the domestic services, but the combined force absorbed these in its enlarged route network. Although the overall international coverage remains largely in the Pacific area, Frankfurt and London are offered as European gateways, while Los Angeles regularly receives the airline's 747s.

FLEET:

Boeing 747-219B: ZK-NZV, ZK-NZW, ZK-NZX, ZK-NZY, ZK-NZZ	
Boeing 747-419: ZK-NBS, ZK-NBT, ZK-NBU, ZK-NBV (on order)	
Boeing 747-441: ZK-SUI	
Boeing 747-475: ZK-SUH	
Also operated are Boeing 737/767s.	

UK airport served: Heathrow.

Air Seychelles (HM/SEY)
PO Box 386, Victoria, Mahé

Seychelles
Tel: 22 53 00

After being formed in September 1977, Air Seychelles was engaged mainly in inter-island flights until a service to London and Frankfurt was started in October 1983. The company leased a DC-10 from British Caledonian at first, but later this was replaced by a similar machine from Martinair. Other types were also employed pending the arrival of the proposed Airbus A310, but eventually it was a pair of hush-kitted Boeing 707s which took over the international schedules in early 1988. A single Boeing 767 was leased at the end of the following year, at which point the 707s were returned to their lessor. The wide-bodied type has since remained with the airline and was joined by a 757 in 1993.

FLEET:

Boeing 757-28A: S7-AAX	
Boeing 767-2Q8ER: S7-AAS	
Boeing 767-37DER: S7-AAZ	

UK airports served: Gatwick and Manchester.

Air South West (8H/PIE)
Exeter Airport, Exeter, Devon

United Kingdom
Tel: (01392) 446447

Known as Newquay Air when formed in May 1993, the airline began by offering a scheduled service from Newquay to Cork. In due course the name Air South West was adopted and the company's headquarters relocated at Exeter which became the UK terminal for both Irish routes. Connections are now made with transatlantic services at Dublin which is now linked thrice daily.

FLEET:

PA-31-350 Navajo Chieftain: G-GRAM

EMB-110P1 Bandeirante: G-BGYT

UK airports served: Belfast, Blackpool, Exeter and Plymouth.

Air Toulouse International (TLE)
BP 44, F-31702 Blagnac

France
Tel: (60) 30 01 22

The airline started operations in December 1990, subsequently concentrating its efforts on charter flights from its home base at Toulouse. It has become one of the last operators using the Caravelle for passenger work, although the three on strength have now been joined by Boeing 737s.

FLEET:

Boeing 737-2D6: F-GLXH

Boeing 737-2M8: F-GLXG

Boeing 737-2S3: F-GHXL

Boeing 737-219: F-GLXF

SE210 Caravelle 10B3: F-BMKS, F-GELP, F-GHMU

UK airports served: Birmingham and Luton.

Below: **F-GHXL — Boeing 737-2S3 of Air Toulouse.**

Air Transat (TS/TSC)　　　Canada
905 Boulevard Michèle-Bohec, Blainville, Québec　　Tel: (514) 433 10 11

Formed in December 1986, Air Transat began operations from Montreal in November 1987 and Toronto in April 1988. The airline is now Canada's largest charter carrier with services to Central and South America, the Caribbean, Europe and the US.

FLEET:

Boeing 757-23A: C-GTSE, C-GTSF
Boeing 757-28A: C-GTSN
Boeing 757-236: C-GTSJ
L1011-385 TriStar 1: C-FWCR, C-GTSX, C-FTNL
L1011-385 TriStar 100: C-GTSY, C-GTSZ
L1011-385 TriStar 150: C-FTNA, C-FTNB, C-FTNC, C-FTNH
Also operated are Boeing 727s.

UK airports served: Belfast, Birmingham, Cardiff, Edinburgh, Exeter, Gatwick, Glasgow, Leeds/Bradford, Manchester, Newcastle and Stansted.

Above: **C-FTNB — L1011-385 TriStar 150 of Air Transat.**

Air UK (UK/UKA)　　United Kingdom
Stansted House, Stansted Airport, Essex　　Tel: (01279) 660400

The airline was formed on 16 January 1980 by the merger of Air Anglia and British Island Airways, themselves having absorbed Air Wales and Air Westward respectively a few months earlier. Amalgamating two established organisations is never easy, since there is invariably duplication of effort and different managerial opinions to resolve. Added to these early problems was the current

Above: **G-UKFI — Fokker 100 of Air UK.**

recession, so it was not long before the large network inherited began to shrink as the uneconomic routes were axed.

Slowly, the situation improved with visible signs of growth becoming apparent by the mid-1980s. Air UK also increased its presence at Stansted, which by this time was earmarked as London's third airport. Although turboprop types were the mainstay of the airline's fleet, both the Fokker F-28 and One-Eleven were employed at various times during the decade. However, in December 1987 the BAe 146 was introduced into the fleet, to become the first in the long-term modernisation programme. Subsequently this type and the Fokker 100 have become responsible for the growing number of domestic and international routes flown. The faithful and long-serving Friendship 200s were finally replaced by the Fokker 50 in 1994, the year in which Air UK made a profit of over £2.5 million. It is now Britain's third-largest scheduled airline and offers over 1,500 flights each week from a total of 15 UK airports.

FLEET:

BAe 146-100:	G-UKJF
BAe 146-300:	G-BSNR, G-BSNS, G-BTTP, G-BUHC, G-UKAC, G-UKAG, G-UKHP, G-UKID, G-UKRC, G-UKSC
Fokker 50:	G-UKTA, G-UKTB, G-UKTC, G-UKTD, G-UKTE, G-UKTF, G-UKTG, G-UKTH, G-UKTI
Fokker 100:	G-UKFA, G-UKFB, G-UKFC, G-UKFD, G-UKFE, G-UKFF, G-UKFG, G-UKFH, G-UKFI, G-UKFJ, G-UKFK, G-UKFL, G-, G-, G-, G-, G-, G-
F27 Friendship 500:	G-BMXD, G-BNCY, G-BVOB, G-BVOM, G-BVRN
F27 Friendship 600:	G-BNAL

UK airports served: Aberdeen, Edinburgh, Gatwick, Glasgow, Guernsey, Heathrow, Humberside,Inverness, Jersey, Leeds/Bradford, London City, Manchester, Newcastle, Norwich, Southampton, Stansted and Teesside.

Air Zimbabwe (UM/AZW)   Zimbabwe
PO Box AP1, Harare Airport, Harare   Tel: (4) 73 70 11

Central African Airways for many years provided the air transport services for Northern and Southern Rhodesia and Nyasaland, but in 1967 the carrier became government controlled and at the same time adopted Air Rhodesia as its new identity. The airline suffered severe restrictions to its growth during the quest for independence, but once the country's status had been resolved, rapid expansion became possible. Taking the name of Air Zimbabwe, the airline became the national carrier for the newly-created republic in April 1980. Although particular attention was given to the provision of links with neighbouring countries, both domestic and international scheduled flights were also developed. Joint services are operated to Perth and Sydney in association with Qantas, the equipment being one of the Australian carrier's 747s

FLEET:

Boeing 707-330B: Z-WKS, Z-WKU

Boeing 767-2N0ER: Z-WPE, Z-WPF

Also operated are three Boeing 737s, one BAe 146-200 and two Fokker 50s.

UK airport served: Gatwick.

Air 2000 (DP/AMM)   United Kingdom
First Choice House, Crawley, West Sussex   Tel: (01293) 518966

Operations were commenced by the Manchester-based airline in April 1987 using a pair of Boeing 757s. Subsequently the fleet has grown considerably, helping the carrier to become the third-largest charter operator in the UK. It is the in-house airline for First Choice Holidays (previously Owners Abroad), but is also contracted by numerous other companies to provide the transport facilities for their customers. In addition to the traditional routes to the Mediterranean and Canary Islands, Air 2000 also undertakes long-haul trips. These include transatlantic sorties to Canada, the Caribbean and the US, together with flights

Below: **G-OOOU — Boeing 757-2Y0 of Air 2000.**

to The Gambia and Kenya. The airline entered the scheduled service market in October 1993 when Gatwick was regularly linked with Larnaca and Paphos. In May 1994 a similar operation was inaugurated at Birmingham.

FLEET:

Airbus A320-231: G-OOAA, G-OOAB, G-OOAC, G-OOAD	
Boeing 757-2Y0: G-OOOU, G-OOOX	
Boeing 757-23A: G-OOOG, G-OOOI, G-OOOJ	
Boeing 757-28A: G-OOOA, G-OOOB, G-OOOC, G-OOOD	
Boeing 757-225: G-OOOM, G-OOOV, G-OOOW	
Boeing 757-236: G-OOOS, G-OOOT	

UK airports served: Aberdeen, Belfast, Birmingham, Bristol, Cardiff, East Midlands, Exeter, Gatwick, Glasgow, Leeds/Bradford, Luton, Manchester, Newcastle, Stansted and Teesside.

Airtours International Airways (VZ/AIH)

United Kingdom

Parkway 3, 300 Princess Road, Manchester

Tel: (0161) 232 6600

Above: **G-RJGR — Boeing 757-225 of Airtours International.**

The Airtours Group set up its own in-house airline in the early 1990s, with operations beginning at Manchester in March 1991. Initially, the airline was equipped with MD83s, but with the acquisition of Aspro Holidays and its associated airline, Inter European, different types have joined the fleet. These included the Boeing 757 and Airbus A320, the latter becoming the standard equipment by replacing the MD83s in 1995/96. Two Boeing 767s were acquired in 1994 to handle the long-haul commitments which include charters to the Caribbean, the US and Australia.

FLEET:

Airbus A320-212: G-DACR, G-DRVE, G-HBAP, G-JANM, G-JDFW, G-RRJE, G-TPTT
Airbus A320-231: G-CRPH, G-SUEE, G-YJBM
Boeing 757-23A: G-LCRC
Boeing 757-225: G-JALC, G-MCEA, G-PIDS, G-RJGR, G-
Boeing 757-236: G-CSVS
Boeing 767-31KER: G-DAJC, G-SJMC

UK airports served: Belfast, Birmingham, Bristol, Cardiff, East Midlands, Gatwick, Glasgow, Humberside, Leeds/Bradford, Manchester, Newcastle and Stansted.

Airworld (AWD)   United Kingdom
25 Elmfield Road, Bromley, Kent   Tel: (0181) 325 3200

The UK tour operator Iberotravel decided to create its own airline after Inter European was absorbed by Airtours. Operations began at Manchester in April 1994, with charters from Bristol commencing several days later. At the end of the summer season the airline suspended its activities for the duration of the winter, but after the restart in 1995 Airworld planned to continue throughout the year.

FLEET:

Airbus A320-231: G-BVJV, G-BVJW, G-BVZU

UK airports served: Bristol, Cardiff, East Midlands, Gatwick, Glasgow and Manchester.

Alitalia (AZ/AZA)   Italy
Palazzo Alitalia, Piazzale Guillo Pastore,
I-00144 Rome   Tel: (6) 54 441

Unlike Germany, Italy's air transport activities were allowed to restart at an early date after the war. On 16 September 1946 Aerolinee Italiane Internazionali was formed with the backing of BEA. A second airline known as Linee Aeree Italiane (LAI) was also launched on that day, this time with the support of TWA. During the next 10 years or so a comprehensive network of domestic and international routes was built up. While there was a certain amount of overlap between the two companies, this was not considered too important at first since most of the Middle and Far East, Africa and South America were served by only one carrier. However, in due course the duplication became unacceptable, so in 1957 it was decreed that the two should merge and adopt the identity of Alitalia.

After a period of rationalisation the new airline emerged with a fleet of DC-7s for the US routes, with the European services using DC-3s, DC-6s, Viscounts and Convair 440s. Two years later the jet age reached Italy to mark the start of a new period for the airline. Caravelles and DC-8s began to replace the piston-engined types, although by the end of the 1960s the DC-9 was

Above: **I-BIXU — Airbus A321-112 of Alitalia.** *A. S. Wright*

becoming the mainstay of the short-haul fleet, supported later by Boeing 727s.
During the next decade further expansion brought the DC-10 and Boeing 747
into use, while Airbus A300s were acquired in the early 1980s. After another
standardisation exercise the DC-8 was phased out, the DC-10s sold and a start
made on the DC-9 and 727 replacement programme by the MD-80 series
aircraft. In 1995, the remaining DC-9s slowly continued to leave the fleet, their
place taken by the Airbus A321, deliveries being spread over a number of years.
The company absorbed its subsidiary (ATI) during 1995, but a year later Alitalia
announced plans to split the airline into two divisions, one to handle longhaul
operations with medium and short-haul flights becoming the responsibility of
the second.

FLEET:

Airbus A300B2-203: I-BUSM, I-BUSN

Airbus A300B4-103: I-BUSP, I-BUSQ, I-BUSR, I-BUST

Airbus A300B4-203: I-BUSB, I-BUSC, I-BUSD, I-BUSF, I-BUSG, I-BUSH, I-BUSJ,
I-BUSL

Airbus A321-112: I-BIXA, I-BIXB, I-BIXC, I-BIXD, I-BIXE, I-BIXF, I-BIXG, I-BIXI,
I-BIXL, I-BIXM, I-BIXN, I-BIXO, I-BIXP, I-BIXQ, I-BIXR, I-BIXS, I-BIXT, I-BIXU,
I-BIXV, I-BIXZ

Boeing 747-230B: I-DEMY

Boeing 747-243B: I-DEMC, I-DEMD, I-DEMF, I-DEMG, I-DEML, I-DEMP, I-DEMS,
I-DEMV

Boeing 747-243F: I-DEMR

Boeing 767-33AER: G-OITA, G-OITB, G-OITC, G-OITF, G-OITG, G-OITL

Douglas DC-9-32: I-DIBI, I-DIKM, I-DIKR, I-DIZE, I-RIFE, I-RIFJ, I-RIFL,
I-RIFS, I-RIFT, I-RIFU, I-RIFV, I-RIFW, I-RIFY

McD Douglas MD11: I-DUPA, I-DUPB, I-DUPC, I-DUPD, I-DUPE, I-DUPI,
I-DUPO, I-DUPU

McD Douglas MD82: I-DACM, I-DACN, I-DACP, I-DACQ, I-DACR, I-DACS, I-DACT,
I-DACU, I-DACV, I-DACW, I-DACX, I-DACY, I-DACZ, I-DAND, I-DANF, I-DANG,
I-DANH, I-DANL, I-DANP, I-DANQ, I-DANR, I-DANU, I-DANV, I-DANW, I-DATA,

I-DATB,	I-DATC,	I-DATD,	I-DATE,	I-DATF,	I-DATG,	I-DATH,	I-DATI,	I-DATJ,
I-DATK,	I-DATL,	I-DATM,	I-DATN,	I-DATO,	I-DATP,	I-DATQ,	I-DATR,	I-DATS,
I-DATT,	I-DATU,	I-DATV,	I-DATW,	I-DATX,	I-DATY,	I-DAVA,	I-DAVB,	I-DAVC,
I-DAVD,	I-DAVF,	I-DAVG,	I-DAVH,	I-DAVI,	I-DAVJ,	I-DAVK,	I-DAVL,	I-DAVM,
I-DAVN,	I-DAVP,	I-DAVR,	I-DAVS,	I-DAVT,	I-DAVU,	I-DAVV,	I-DAVW,	I-DAVX,
I-DAVZ,	I-DAWA,	I-DAWB,	I-DAWC,	I-DAWD,	I-DAWE,	I-DAWF,	I-DAWG,
I-DAWH,	I-DAWI,	I-DAWJ,	I-DAWL,	I-DAWM,	I-DAWO,	I-DAWP,	I-DAWQ,
I-DAWR,	I-DAWS,	I-DAWT,	I-DAWU,	I-DAWV,	I-DAWW,	I-DAWY,	I-DAWZ

UK airports served: Gatwick and Heathrow.

All Leisure Airlines (ALT) — United Kingdom
26 Upper Fitzwilliam Street, Dublin 2 — Tel (1) 662 18 88

The airline was formed to operate IT charters and holds a 49% interest in the Irish company TransLift. Joint operation of the latter's fleet has resulted in one aircraft being transferred to the UK register.

FLEET:

Airbus A320-231: G-OALA

All Nippon Airways (NH/ANA) — Japan
2-5 Kasumigaseki, 3-Chome, Chiyoda-ku,
Tokyo 100 — Tel: (3) 580 47 11

A merger between Nippon Helicopters and Far East Airlines in March 1958 produced All Nippon Airways. Through the years the carrier has grown to become Japan's largest domestic carrier with more than a 50% share of the market. Despite its size the airline was not well known outside its homeland before international schedules were introduced in 1986 when a Boeing 747 linked Tokyo with Guam. After this cautious start, ANA introduced a non-stop service to Los Angeles in July, a sector already flown by Japan Airlines and six other carriers. The first European service operated by the company's own aircraft was launched in July 1989 when three weekly visits were made to London/Gatwick. By the time that the UK gateway was moved to Heathrow in July 1991 the total number of weekly departures had reached six and by the end of the year the target of a daily non-stop service had been reached. Boeing 747-400s have subsequently taken over the duties from the earlier Series 200s.

FLEET:

Boeing 747-281B: JA8174, JA8175, JA8181, JA8182, JA8190

Boeing 747-2D3B: JA8192

Boeing 747-481: JA8094, JA8095, JA8096, JA8097, JA8098, JA8958, JA8962

Also operated are Airbus A320s, Boeing 747SRs and Boeing 767s.

On order: Airbus A340 and Boeing 777.

UK airport served: Heathrow.

American Airlines (AA/AAL)

USA

PO Box 619616, DFW International Airport,
Dallas, Tx

Tel: (817) 967 12 34

American Airlines was formed in 1934 by the amalgamation of numerous small carriers. Its interests spread far and wide across the United States, reaching from the Pacific to the Atlantic coast. An international career almost started in 1942 when the airline was awarded the Dallas–Mexico route, but wartime restrictions prevented the launch until hostilities had ceased. Through the years American has contributed much to the design of several airliners including the Convair 240 and 990, Lockheed Electra and Douglas DC-3, DC-7, DC-10 and MD11. As one of the world's largest carriers in all respects, its flight operations criss-cross the US and take in Hawaii, the Caribbean islands, Mexico and Canada. A transatlantic route was opened in May 1982 to link Dallas with London, but the carrier considerably increased its presence when it bought 12 routes from TWA in 1991. As a result, many of the major European cities were added to the network.

FLEET:

Boeing **757-223ET**: N687AA, N688AA, N689AA, N690AA, N691AA, N692AA

Boeing **767-223ER**: N312AA, N313AA, N315AA, N316AA, N317AA, N319AA,
  N320AA, N321AA, N322AA, N323AA, N324AA, N325AA, N327AA, N328AA,
  N329AA, N330AA, N332AA, N334AA, N335AA, N336AA, N338AA, N339AA

Boeing **767-323ER**: N351AA, N352AA, N353AA, N354AA, N355AA, N357AA,
  N358AA, N359AA, N36OAA, N361AA, N362AA, N363AA, N366AA, N368AA,
  N369AA, N370AA, N371AA, N372AA, N373AA, N374AA, N376AN, N377AN,
  N378AN, N379AA, N380AN, N381AN, N382AN, N383AN, N384AA, N385AM,
  N386AA, N387AM, N388AA, N389AA, N390AA, N391AA, N7375A, N39356,
  N39364, N39365, N39367

McD Douglas **MD11**: N1750B, N1752K, N1754, N1755, N1756,
  N1757A, N1758B, N1759, N1760A, N1761R, N1762B, N1763, N1764B, N1765B,
  N1766A, N1767A, N1768D

Also operated are Airbus A300-605Rs, Boeing 727/757s, Douglas DC-10s,
  Fokker 100s, McD Douglas MD82s and MD83s.

UK airports served: Birmingham, Gatwick, Glasgow, Heathrow and Manchester.

American International Airways (CB/CKS)

USA

842 Willow Run Airport, Ypsilanti, Mi 48197

Tel: (313) 484 00 88

Previously known as Connie Kalitta Services, the renamed airline undertakes both passenger and cargo charters together with regular contract work for the overnight parcel industry. A collection of DC-8 variants make up the fleet, but a growing number of Boeing 747s and TriStars are being introduced.

FLEET:

Boeing 747-146F: N701CK, N702CK, N703CK, N704CK	
Boeing 747-238B: N706CK	
Douglas DC-8-51: N804CK, N805CK	
Douglas DC-8-52: N810CK	
Douglas DC-8-54: N802CK, N806CK	
Douglas DC-8-55: N801CK, N807CK, N808CK	
Douglas DC-8-61: N812CK, N813CK, N816CK, N817CK	
Douglas DC-8-63: N811CK, N815CK	
L1011-385 TriStar 50: N112CK	
L1011-385 TriStar 200: N105CK, N102CK, N103CK, N104CK, N106CK	

UK airports served: None regularly.

American Trans Air (TZ/AMT)   USA
PO Box 51609, Indianapolis, In 46251   Tel: (317) 247 40 00

Domestic and international passenger charter services were started in March 1981, although the airline flew on behalf of the Ambassador Travel Club from 1973. Several Boeing 727s were acquired, while the long-haul operations were handled by 707s. This equipment was intended to be an interim arrangement in view of the forthcoming US noise regulations. The first of the replacements proved to be a DC-10 in 1983, but subsequently the carrier decided to standardise on the TriStar instead since a number of ex-Delta machines were available. A number of scheduled services are now flown, while the fleet has included the Boeing 757 since the beginning of the 1990s.

Above: **N186AT — L1011-385 TriStar 50 of American Trans Air.**

FLEET:

Boeing 757-23A: N512AT	
Boeing 757-23N: N514AT, N515AT, N516AT, N517AT, N518AT, N519AT, N520AT	
Boeing 757-2Q8: N754AT, N755AT, N756AT	
L1011-385 TriStar 1: N176AT, N179AT, N183AT	
L1011-385 TriStar 50: N185AT, N186AT, N187AT, N188AT, N189AT, N190AT, N191AT, N192AT, N193AT, N196AT, N197AT	
L1011-385 TriStar 100: N181AT, N194AT	
L1011-385 TriStar 150: N195AT	
Boeing 727s are also operated.	

UK airport served: Gatwick.

AOM French Airlines (IW/AOM)　　France

BP 23, Aéroport Nîmes-Aries-Camargue,
F-30128 Garons　　Tel: (1) 49 79 10 00

The airline was created by the merger of Minerve and Air Outre Mer in January 1992. A number of long-haul scheduled services are flown by the large fleet of DC-10s, while MD83s are employed on domestic sectors and charter work to the Mediterranean holiday areas.

FLEET:

Douglas DC-10-30: F-BTDD, F-BTDE, F-GHOI, F-GKMY, F-GLMX, F-GNDC, F-GNEM, F-GTDF, F-GTDG, F-GTDI, F-ODLX, F-ODLY, F-ODLZ	
McD Douglas MD11: F- , F-	
McD Douglas MD83: F-GGMA, F-GGMB, F-GGMC, F-GGMD, F-GGME, F-GGMF, F-GRMC, F-GRMG, F-GRMH, F-GRMI, F-GRMJ	

UK airports served: None regularly

Arrow Air (JW/APW)　　USA

PO Box 026062, Miami, Fl 33102　　Tel: (305) 526 09 00

Originally set up in 1947, the airline has had several changes of policy since that time. Nowadays cargo and passenger charters are undertaken, the latter after an absence from such operations in the period from 1986 to 1993.

FLEET:

Douglas DC-8-62F: N802BN, N810BN, N1803, N1804	
Douglas DC-8-63F: N345JW, N441J, N661AV	
L1011-385 TriStar 200: N306GB, N308GB	

UK airports served: None regularly.

Atlas Air Cargo (5Y/GTI) USA

Building 263, JFK International, NY 11430-1812   Tel: (718) 656 40 00

The all-747 cargo carrier was formed in 1992 to provide services on behalf of the major airlines around the world. It has since acquired a number of combi 747s with the intention of converting them to all-cargo configuration with a high gross weight. It is anticipated that the company will be operating 24 examples of the type by the end of 1997.

FLEET:

Boeing 747-128F: N3203Y	
Boeing 747-2D3BF: N505MC, N506MC	
Boeing 747-2D7BF: N-, N-, N-, N-, N-, N-	
Boeing 747-2R7F: N639FE	
Boeing 747-212BF: N808MC	
Boeing 747-230BF: N507MC, N508MC, N509MC, N512MC	
Boeing 747-230F: N747MC	
Boeing 747-243BF: N516MC, N517MC, N518MC	
Boeing 747-245F: N636FE, N638FE, N640FE, N641FE	

UK airports served: Gatwick and Heathrow.

Augsburg Airways (IQ/AUB) Germany

Flughafenstrasse 6, D-86169, Augsburg   Tel: (821) 29 09 70

The airline was formed as Interot Airways in the early 1980s to operate business charter flights between its home base and Dusseldorf. These were developed into a scheduled service network within Germany, with the company's first international sector added in the mid-1990s. Links between London City, Cologne and Augsburg began in November 1995 using Dash Eights. The venture proved sufficiently successful for an increase in frequency after a short time.

FLEET:

DHC-8-103 Dash Eight: D-BAGB, D-BIER, D-BIRT
DHC-8-311 Dash Eight: D-BACH
DHC-8-314 Dash Eight: D-BMUC

UK airport served: London City.

Aurigny Air Services (GR/AUR) United Kingdom

Grande Rue, St Martins, Guernsey   Tel: (01481) 35311

Aurigny has been providing rapid and frequent inter-Channel Islands services since April 1968. A pair of Islanders were employed at that time, but by the end of 1970 traffic had risen to such a level that eight of the nine-seaters were in use on the busy schedules. During the next year the airline, realising that larger-capacity aircraft were needed, opted for the 16-seat Trislander. Steadily the new machines replaced the Islanders, although two of the latter were retained for some years.

An attempt to modernise the fleet with the slightly larger and quieter Twin Otter brought two into service in 1980. However, after a fairly short time, it became apparent that the type was not really suited to Aurigny's operations. Both were sold in favour of more of the well-tried Trislanders which are still the mainstay of the fleet. The airline purchased Guernsey Airlines from British Air Ferries in 1987, but soon discontinued most of the latter's scheduled services. In 1990 a Short SD3-60 was acquired to operate charters in addition to flying on the regular routes at peak times.

FLEET:

BN-2A Mk III-2 Trislander: G-BDTN, G-BDWV, G-BEPH, G-BEPI, G-BEVT, G-JOEY, G-OCTA, G-RBSI, G-XTOR	
Short SD3-60: G-OAAS	

UK airports served: Alderney, Bournemouth, East Midlands, Gatwick, Guernsey, Jersey and Southampton.

Austrian Airlines (OS/AUA)　　Austria
Postfach 50, Fontanastrasse 1, A-1107 Wien　　Tel: (1) 683 51 00

Austrian Airlines was formed in September 1957 by the merger of Air Austria and Austrian Airways. Operations started in 1958 using a Viscount leased from Fred Olsen, a company which also provided assistance in the early years.

Caravelles appeared with the carrier in 1963 followed by DC-9s in January 1971. Modernisation of the fleet began in the early 1980s when the stretched

Above: **OE-LDT — McD Douglas MD81 of Austrian Airlines**

MD81 variant of the DC-9 began to replace the older aircraft. The Airbus A310 was chosen for use on the long-haul routes and also for the high density IT charters to the Mediterranean and Canary Islands routes. Tyrolean is an associate company which operates services for the flag carrier.

FLEET:

Airbus A310-324: OE-LAA, OE-LAB, OE-LAC
Airbus A310-325: OE-LAD
Airbus A320-214: OE- , OE- , OE- , OE- , OE-
Airbus A321-111: OE-LBA, OE-LBB, OE-LBC, OE-LBD, OE-LBE, OE-LBF
Airbus A340-212: OE-LAG, OE-LAH
Fokker 70: OE-LFO, OE-LFP, OE-LFQ, OE-LFR, OE-LFS, OE- , OE-
McD Douglas MD81: OE-LDP, OE-LDR, OE-LDS, OE-LDT, OE-LDU, OE-LDV, OE-LDW
McD Douglas MD82: OE-LDX, OE-LDY, OE-LDZ, OE-LMA, OE-LMB, OE-LMC
McD Douglas MD83: OE-LMD, OE-LME
McD Douglas MD87: OE-LMK, OE-LML, OE-LMM, OE-LMN, OE-LMO

UK airport served: Heathrow.

Aviaco (AO/AYC) — Spain
Calle Maudes 51, Edificio Minister, E-28003 Madrid   Tel: (1) 534 42 00

Operations were started in 1948 using Bristol Freighters for cargo charter work. This venture was not particularly successful, so the airline soon turned its attention towards the passenger market. Licences were obtained to operate over a few routes for which the same aircraft were initially employed, albeit suitably converted for their new role. They were replaced in 1952 by some ex-Air France Languedocs which duly took over the existing routes and others

Below: **EC-FPJ — McD Douglas MD88 of Aviaco.**

radiating from Madrid. Gradually more modern types were received, with the Caravelle marking the company's entry into the jet age.

Aviaco also developed into a major charter carrier, securing a large amount of IT work from the UK travel industry in the 1970s and 1980s, but a change of policy later found the airline reverting to mainly scheduled work. Iberia transferred a number of routes to its subsidiary, with much of the charter work taken over by new Spanish airlines formed for the purpose.

FLEET:

Douglas DC-9-32: EC-BIH, EC-BIK, EC-BIP, EC-BIQ, EC-BQY, EC-BYE, EC-BYF, EC-BYI, EC-BYJ, EC-CGN, EC-CGO, EC-CGP, EC-CGQ, EC-CGR, EC-CLD

Douglas DC-9-34: EC-CTR, EC-CTS, EC-CTU, EC-DGC, EC-DGD, EC-DGE

McD Douglas MD88: EC-FGM, EC-FHG, EC-FIG, EC-FIH, EC-FJE, EC-FLK, EC-FLN, EC-FND, EC-FOF, EC-FOG, EC-FOZ, EC-FPD, EC-FPJ

UK airport served: Stansted.

BAC Express (RPX) — United Kingdom
BAC House, Bonehurst Road, Horley, Surrey — Tel: (01293) 821621

Above: G-UBAC — **Short SD3-60 of BAC Express.**

The company was established in 1992 as a part of the BAC Group. *Ad hoc* charters are undertaken, but much of its work is involved with the overnight movement of mail and parcels. However, regular passenger charters are flown between Southend and the Channel Islands during the summer months. The company is also a source of aircraft for other carriers in need of additional capacity.

FLEET:

Herald 214: G-ATIG	
Herald 402: G-BEYK	
Short SD3-30: G-BGNB, G-B10E, G-BIYG, G-BKIE	
Short SD3-60: G-CBAC, G-CLAS, G-OJSY, G-UBAC	
F27-Friendship 500: G-BVZW	

UK airports served: Belfast, Bristol, Cardiff, East Midlands, Edinburgh, Exeter, Gatwick, Jersey, Luton, Newcastle, Southend and Stansted.

Balkan Bulgarian Airlines (LZ/LAZ)   Bulgaria
Sofia Airport, Sofia 1540   Tel: (2) 88 18 00

Bulgaria was one of four countries assisted by the former Soviet Union during the time that air services were being reorganised after the war, although a company had already been set up known as Bulgarshe Vazdusne Sobstenie (BVS). Using the Russian aid, greater progress was made and the joint Bulgarian–Soviet company was renamed TABSO. Its first international project was to establish a route to Budapest, which in due course was extended to Belgrade and Prague. When the airline was trading successfully the Bulgarian government bought the Russian half share, although still leaving the airline with the same equipment. Thereafter a comprehensive network of domestic scheduled services was built up, while most of the major European cities were included in the international coverage. Charter work was undertaken for various tour operators, with UK companies using the airline for its IT flights to the Black Sea holiday areas. In 1991 major structural changes were introduced within the company and a start made on a programme to replace the Russian types with more modern and reliable Western machines.

FLEET:

Airbus A320-231: LZ-ABB, LZ-ABC, LZ-ABD	
Antonov An-12: LZ-BAC, LZ-BAE, LZ-BAF	

Below: **LZ-BTQ —Tupolev Tu-154M of Balkan Bulgarian.**

Boeing 737-53A: LZ-BOA, LZ-BOB, LZ-BOC

Boeing 767-27EER: F-GHGD, F-GHGE

Ilyushin IL-18: LZ-BEA, LZ-BEH, LZ-BEI, LZ-BEU

Tupolev Tu-134A: LZ-TUG, LZ-TUV, LZ-TUZ

Tupolev Tu-154B: LZ-BTA, LZ-BTC, LZ-BTE, LZ-BTF, LZ-BTG, LZ-BTJ, LZ-BTK, LZ-BTL, LZ-BTM, LZ-BTO, LZ-BTP, LZ-BTS, LZ-BTT, LZ-BTU, LZ-BTV

Tupolev Tu-154M: LZ-BTH, LZ-BTI, LZ-BTN, LZ-BTQ, LZ-BTW, LZ-BTX, LZ-BTY

UK airports served: Birmingham, Gatwick, Glasgow, Heathrow, Leeds/Bradford, Manchester, Newcastle and Stansted.

Bangladesh Biman (BG/BBC)   Bangladesh
Biman Bhavan, Motijheel Commercial Area,
Dhaka 1000   Tel: (2) 24 01 51

When Bangladesh was created in 1971 at the expense of East Pakistan, the infant country found itself without air services, necessitating the fairly rapid launch of a national carrier. Bangladesh Biman was established on 4 January 1972 with operations starting one month later. Friendly nations donated aircraft in sufficient quantities for domestic services to resume quite speedily. International links with London were started on a charter basis in March 1972, but after acquiring a motley collection of weary Boeing 707s, schedules were introduced. Since those early days the airline has grown in strength and now employs DC-10s for such services, with Fellowships and BAe ATPs handling the domestic and regional duties.

FLEET:

Airbus A310-325: S2-ADE, S2-ADF

Douglas DC-10-30: S2-ACO, S2-ACP, S2-ACQ, S2-ACR, S2-ADB

UK airports served: Heathrow.

BASE Airlines (5E/BRO)   Netherlands
PO Box 7165, Eindhoven 5605   Tel: (40) 52 32 45

Regional services are flown by the airline using three Jetstreams. Further growth is planned following some recent refinancing, the first additional routes being twice-daily flights between Birmingham and Rotterdam, to be followed by a similar frequency on a service from the Dutch city to Hamburg. BASE is closely associated with Euro Direct Belgium and VLM.

FLEET:

BAe Jetstream 31: PH-KJA, PH-KJB, PH-KJG

UK airports served: Birmingham, Gatwick and Manchester.

Norwegian shipowner Ludvig Braathen first considered operating air services before World War 2, but he had to wait until 1946 before this was possible. Long-range charters were started within Europe and the Middle East, but it was not long before the airline's livery was to be found in the Far East. In 1949 the carrier was awarded a five-year licence for a scheduled run from Oslo to Hong Kong, a journey taking four days of travel by DC-4, but still much faster than the alternative flying boat services. Later the route was extended via Iceland to Caracas in Venezuela, claimed by Braathens at the time to be the longest flight flown in the world. It was at this point that 'SAFE' was added to the company's title, these being the initial letters of South American and Far East.

Braathens' authority to continue its international schedules was withdrawn in 1954 because of the Norwegian government's policy of supporting the national carrier. Instead the company began domestic operations, a pursuit it has since continued to expand. Charter work also absorbs a considerable amount of Braathens' capacity, while ITs are regularly flown to the traditional holiday areas. A change of policy by the authorities has allowed the airline to introduce international schedules once again, often in competition with SAS. Although the airline acquired a pair of Boeing 767s in 1984, the type proved too large for its needs so both were sold in the following year. The Boeing 737 has been the mainstay of the fleet for many years, with Braathens regularly expanding its fleet with the newer models.

FLEET:

Boeing 737-405: LN-BRA, LN-BRB, LN-BRE, LN-BRI, LN-BRP, LN-BRQ

Boeing 737-4Q8: LN-BUB

Boeing 737-505: LN-BRC, LN-BRD, LN-BRF, LN-BRG, LN-BRH, LN-BRJ, LN-BRK, LN-BRM, LN-BRN, LN-BRO, LN-BRR, LN-BRS, LN-BRT, LN-BRU, LN-BRV, LN-BRX, LN-BUA,LN-BUC, LN-BUD, LN-BUE, LN-BUF

UK airports served: Gatwick, Jersey and Newcastle; others are visited occasionally.

After starting as an air-taxi operator with two Aztecs in 1973, the airline has steadily developed into an active regional carrier based at Morlaix in northern France. A network of domestic, regional and international scheduled services are now operated, some of which are on behalf of Air France with the aircraft painted in the flag carrier's livery displaying the title AirInter Express.

FLEET:

Aérospatiale ATR42-300: F-GFJP, F-GGLR, F-GHJE, F-BHPI, F-GHPK, F-GHPS, F-GHPX, F-GHPZ, F-GKNH, F-GLIA, F-GLIB

Aérospatiale ATR72-201: F-GHPU, F-GHPV, F-GHPY
Canadair Regional Jet: F-GRJA, F-GRJB, F-GRJC, F-GRJD, F-GRJE, F-GRJF
SAAB SF340A: F-GELG, F-GFBZ, F-GHDB, F-GHMI, F-GHMJ, F-GHMK

UK airports served: Bristol, Gatwick and Southampton.

Above: **F-GHMI — SAAB SF340A of Brit Air.** *A. S. Wright*

Britannia Airways (BY/BAL) — United Kingdom
London Luton Airport, Bedfordshire   Tel: (01582) 421455

As a part of the Thomson Organisation, Britannia Airways has become Britain's largest IT carrier with more than 7.5 million passengers carried annually. When formed in 1961 by Universal Sky Tours, it traded as Euravia, but this was changed to its present title in 1964 when the airline began to re-equip with a number of ex-BOAC Britannias. Complete control was gained by Thomsons in the following year and after the first Boeing 737 had been delivered in 1968, the carrier steadily grew, until at the peak, over 30 of the baby Boeings were operated. The company selected the 767 as its new generation equipment with two examples joining the fleet in 1984, with a further pair arriving during the next year. A start was made on the gradual phasing out of the 737s in the mid-1980s, but it was not until 1994 that the last example left the airline. In the meantime the airline absorbed Orion Airways in 1988 which added a number of the more advanced 737-300s, but it was decided to dispose of this variant since in the long term the carrier needed a larger type. Eventually it was the Boeing 757 which entered service in some numbers to become the mainstay of the airline's operations, backed up by the 767s. The latter are also used for long-haul charters which include transatlantic flights and sorties to Australia. For a time Britannia operated a number of scheduled flights, but it is no longer involved in this activity.

Above: **G-BRIF — Boeing 767-204ER of Britannia Airways.**

FLEET:

Boeing 757-204: G-BYAC, G-BYAD, G-BYAE, G-BYAF, G-BYAG, G-BYAH, G-BYAI, G-BYAJ, G-BYAK, G-BYAL, G-BYAN, G-BYAO, G-BYAP, G-BYAR, G-BYAS, G-BYAT, G-BYAU, G-BYAW	
Boeing 757-2T7: G-BYAM	
Boeing 767-204: G-BKPW,	
Boeing 767-204ER: G-BNYS, G-BOPB, G-BRIF, G-BRIG, G-BYAA, G-BYAB	
Boeing 767-304ER: G-OBYA, G-OBYB, G-OBYC, G-OBYD	

UK airports served: Aberdeen, Belfast, Birmingham, Bristol, Cardiff, East Midlands, Edinburgh, Gatwick, Glasgow, Jersey, Leeds/Bradford, Luton, Manchester, Newcastle, Norwich, Stansted and Teesside.

British Airways (BA/BAW)　　　United Kingdom
PO Box 10, Speedbird House,
Heathrow Airport, Hounslow　　　Tel: (0181) 759 5511

The national carrier was created on 1 April 1972 to take control of British Overseas Airways and British European Airways. A number of subsidiaries such as Cambrian and Northeast were also acquired, each gradually losing its individual identity in the process. British Airways is now one of the world's leading international carriers, with a network comprising over 175 destinations in 75 countries. A development in recent times has been the award of a number of franchises for the operation of feeder services as BA Express. Companies selected include CityFlyer, Loganair, GB Airways, Sun-Air of Scandinavia, Maersk Air Ltd and Manx. Investments have been made in Qantas and USAir in order to further the ambition of worldwide coverage, while the airline also has holdings in Brymon (100%), GB Airways (49%), TAT European (49%), Deutsche BA (49%) and Air Mauritius (12.77%).

A successful flotation on the stock exchange was made in 1987, the year in which it acquired the Gatwick-based British Caledonian Airways. The charter element of the company was renamed Caledonian Airways and merged with British Airtours, the existing company specialising in IT work for the flag carrier. In October 1992 BA bought the failed Dan-Air, incorporating the latter's scheduled operations into an expanded Gatwick organisation.

FLEET:

Airbus A320-111: G-BUSB, G-BUSC, G-BUSD, G-BUSE, G-BUSF, G-BUSG, G-BUSH, G-BUSI, G-BUSJ, G-BUSK

BAe ATP: G-BTPA, G-BTPC, G-BTPD, G-BTPE, G-BTPF, G-BTPG, G-BTPH, G-BTPI, G-BTPJ, G-BTPK, G-BTPL, G-BTPM, G-BTPN, G-BTPO, G-BUWP

Boeing 737-236: G-BGDA, G-BGDB, G-BGDE, G-BGDF, G-BGDG, G-BGDI, G-BGDJ, G-BGDK, G-BGDL, G-BGDO, G-BGDP, G-BGDR, G-BGDT, G-BGJE, G-BGJF, G-BGJH, G-BGJI, G-BGJJ, G-BKYA, G-BKYB, G-BKYC, G-BKYE, G-BKYF, G-BKYG, G-BKYH, G-BKYI, G-BKYJ, G-BKYK, G-BJYL, G-BKYM, G-BKYN, G-BKYO, G-BKYP

Boeing 737-4Q8: G-BSNV, G-BSNW, G-BUHJ, G-BUHK

Boeing 737-4S3: G-BVNM, G-BVNN, G-BVNO

Boeing 737-436: G-BVBY, G-BVHB, G-DOCA, G-DOCB, G-DOCC, G-DOCD, G-DOCE, G-DOCF, G-DOCG, G-DOCH, G-DOCI, G-DOCJ, G-DOCK, G-DOCL, G-DOCM, G-DOCN, G-DOCO, G-DOCP, G-DOCR, G-DOCS, G-DOCT, G-DOCU, G-DOCV, G-DOCW, G-DOCX, G-DOCZ, G-GBTA,

Boeing 747-136: G-AWNA, G-AWNB, G-AWNC, G-AWNE, G-AWNF, G-AWNG, G-AWNH, G-AWNJ, G-AWNL, G-AWNM, G-AWNN, G-AWNO, G-AWNP, G-BBPU, G-BDPV

Boeing 747-236B: G-BDXA, G-BDXB, G-BDXC, G-BDXD, G-BDXE, G-BDXF, G-BDXG, G-BDXH, G-BDXI, G-BDXJ, G-BDXK, G-BDXL, G-BDXM, G-BDXN, G-BDXO, G-BDXP

Boeing 747-436: G-BNLA, G-BNLB, G-BNLC, G-BNLD, G-BNLE, G-BNLF, G-BNLG,

Above: **G-BNLB — Boeing 747-436 of British Airways.**

G-BNLH, G-BNLI, G-BNLJ, G-BNLK, G-BNLL, G-BNLM, G-BNLN, G-BNLO,
G-BNLP, G-BNLR, G-BNLS, G-BNLT, G-BNLU, G-BNLV, G-BNLW, G-BNLX,
G-BNLY, G-BNLZ, G-CIVA, G-CIVB, G-CIVC, G-CIVD, G-CIVE, G-CIVF, G-CIVG,
G-CIVH, G-CIVI, G-CIVJ, G-CIVK, G-CIVL

Boeing 757-236: G-BIKA, G-BIKB, G-BIKC, G-BIKD, G-BIKE, G-BIKF, G-BIKG, G-BIKH,
G-BIKI, G-BIKJ, G-BIKK, G-BIKL, G-BIKM, G-BIKN, G-BIKO, G-BIKP, G-BIKR,
G-BIKS, G-BIKT, G-BIKU, G-BIKV, G-BIKW, G-BIKX, G-BIKY, G-BIKZ, G-BMRA,
G-BMRB, G-BMRC, G-BMRD, G-BMRE, G-BMRF, G-BMRG, G-BMRH, G-BMRI,
G-BMRJ, G-BPEA, G-BPEB, G-BPEC, G-BPED, G-BPEE, G-BPEF, G-BPEI, G-BPEJ,
G-BPEK, G-CPEL

Boeing 767-336ER: G-BNWA, G-BNWB, G-BNWC, G-BNWD, G-BNWE, G-BNWF,
G-BNWG, G-BNWH, G-BNWI, G-BNWJ, G-BNWK, G-BNWL, G-BNWM,
G-BMWN, G-BNWO. G-BNWP, G-BNWR, G-BNWS, G-BNWT, G-BNWU,
G-BNWV, G-BNWW, G-BNWX, G-BNWY, G-BNWZ

Boeing 777-236: G-VIIA, G-VIIB, G-VIIC, G-VIID, G-VIIE, G-VIFF, G-VIIG, G-VIIIH,
G-VIIJ, G-RAES, G-ZZZA, G-ZZZB, G-ZZZC, G-ZZZD, G-ZZZE

Concorde 102: G-BOAA, G-BOAB, G-BOAC, G-BOAD, G-BOAE, G-BOAF

Douglas DC-10-30: G-BEBL, G-BEBM, G-BHDH, G-BHDI, G-BHDJ, G-DCIO, G-MULL

UK airports served: Aberdeen, Belfast, Benbecula, Birmingham, Edinburgh, Gatwick, Glasgow, Heathrow, Inverness, Jersey, Kirkwall, Manchester, Newcastle, Stornoway and Sumburgh.

British Mediterranean Airways (KJ/LAS) United Kingdom
53 Mount Street, Mayfair, London   Tel: (0171) 493 3030

The airline was formed in 1994, with operations starting on 28 October using a single Airbus A320 for a five-times-per-week scheduled service between Gatwick and Beirut. It is expected that the network will be expanded to include other destinations in the Middle East area.

FLEET:
Airbus A320-231: G-MEDA

UK airport served: Gatwick.

British Midland Airways (BD/BMA) United Kingdom
Donington Hall, Castle Donington, Leicestershire   Tel: (01332) 854040

When Derby Aviation began scheduled services in 1953, the first routes were seasonal links with the Channel Islands, but it was not long before IT flights were being operated for Midlands tour operators. A change of name to Derby Airways in 1959 encouraged more expansion. which in due course included the arrival of three DC-4Ms specifically for the growing charter business. On 1 October 1964, the airline formally adopted its present title shortly after taking delivery of its first turboprop type, a Herald. April 1965 saw British Midland take up residence at the new East Midlands airport, where all

Above: **G-OBMH — Boeing 737-33A of British Midland Airways.**

operations were then centred. The first of many Viscounts arrived in 1967, a type which subsequently became the mainstay of the fleet for many years. Entry into the transatlantic business brought a Boeing 707 into the fold, while three One-Elevens were acquired for European charter work in 1970.

This latter type did not remain for long since a change of policy took the airline out of this competitive market in order to concentrate on scheduled services. As a result, a whole fleet of Viscounts was bought in South Africa, these aircraft being joined by some Heralds for use on the thinner routes. A profitable leasing division began offering 707s to other operators for short- or long-term periods, many of the customers being the newly-formed African states' national carriers. Jet equipment returned to the fleet in the late 1970s, but this time it was the DC-9 which was chosen.

Nowadays British Midland operates an extensive network of domestic and international scheduled services and is now one of the UK's leading carriers, second only to BA in terms of passengers carried. In addition, there is a limited involvement in IT charters using either the 737-300 or Series 400 aircraft. A major fleet modernisation programme in 1993 brought the first 737-500s into the fleet, while an agreement was also signed for the long-term lease of four Fokker 100s and five Fokker 70s. These replaced the carrier's DC-9s, the last example being withdrawn in April 1996.

FLEET:

Boeing 737-33A: G-OBMD, G-OBMH, G-OBMJ	
Boeing 737-3Q8: G-OBML, G-OBMP	
Boeing 737-4S3: G-OBMK	
Boeing 737-4Y0: G-OBMF, G-OBMG, G-OBMM	
Boeing 737-46B: G-OBMN	
Boeing 737-4Q8: G-OBMO	
Boeing 737-53A: G-OBMZ	
Boeing 737-59D: G-BVKA, G-BVKB, G-BVKC, G-BVKD, G-BVZE, G-BVZF,	

G-OBMX, G-OBMY

Boeing 737-5Q8: G-BVZG, G-BVZH, G-BVZI

Boeing 737-5YO: G-OBMR

Fokker 70: G-BVTE, G-BVTF, G-BVTG, G-BVTH, G- , G-

Fokker 100: G-BVJA, G-BVJB, G-BVJC, G-BVJD

UK airports served: Aberdeen, Belfast, Birmingham, East Midlands, Edinburgh, Gatwick, Glasgow, Guernsey, Heathrow, Jersey, Leeds/Bradford and Teesside.

British World Airlines (VF/BWL) United Kingdom
Viscount House, Southend Airport, Essex · Tel: (01702) 354435

Few UK airlines can claim a career of some 50 years, but British World, with the help of its forebears, has this distinction. Silver City started the car ferry business in 1948, a service which later became the responsibility of British United Air Ferries and British Air Ferries. When this employment was ended in the mid-1970s, the airline turned to charter work and leased out its large Herald fleet. Scheduled services were also introduced in this period, but the operation plus a number of aircraft were transferred to British Island.

When British Airways retired its Viscount fleet in the early 1980s many of them passed to BAF. After refurbishment the aircraft were then leased for short- and long-term periods, but new ownership for the company changed the policy once again. It was decided to re-enter the scheduled scene and for several years the Channel Islands routes in particular were well served by BAF's Viscounts. However, not all the services were profitable and by 1987 such activity ceased and the company was placed in Administration.

Eventually the airline emerged from this situation to continue its charter and leasing work with no intention of becoming involved in schedules. Yet another change in management brought a different viewpoint and with it came the decision to ply routes not currently served. Bucharest became the first in this category in 1993, but the thrice-weekly One-Eleven link was not particularly successful so was quietly dropped in the following year. In the meantime, the airline had changed its name to British World, at the same time introducing an unusual livery for its fleet. Its charter operations were expanded with the acquisition of a number of ex-Dan-Air One-Elevens, while the 146 was also introduced. Until the delivery of two ATR72s in 1996, three members of the Viscount fleet were permanently based at Aberdeen to maintain the Sumburgh flights for the oil industry, but with one exception, the examples of the type that remain operational have been repainted in a red livery for the benefit of Parcelforce. Stansted is now the main operational base, with Southend used for engineering and administration.

FLEET:

Aérospatiale ATR 72-212: G-OILA, G-OILB

BAC One-Eleven 518FG: G-OBWA, G-OBWB, G-OBWD

BAC One-Eleven 520FN: G-OBWC

BAC One-Eleven 531FS: G-OBWE

BAe 146-300: G-BTZN

V802 Viscount: G-AOHM, G-OPFI
V806 Viscount: G-APEY, G-PFBT
V836 Viscount: G-BFZL

UK airports served: Aberdeen, Belfast, Birmingham, Coventry, Edinburgh, Exeter, Gatwick, Liverpool, Manchester, Southend, Stansted, Sumburgh; and others as necessary for charters.

Brymon Airways (BC/BRY) — United Kingdom
City Airport, Crownhill, Plymouth — Tel: (01752) 705151

Brymon began its operations in 1969 when it took over the activities of the Fairoaks School of Flying, but the new company soon began seasonal services in the West Country with an Islander. This type rapidly proved itself to be too small, so the airline became the first UK operator of the Twin Otter, a machine well suited to the small fields used at Land's End and the Scilly Isles. A big step was taken in 1977 when the Newquay–Heathrow schedule was taken over from British Midland. A Herald was used for the route with considerable success, but in 1982 it gave way to the Dash Seven, three of which were in service with the carrier by this time.

It was with this type that Brymon became associated with the London STOLport project, which eventually became operational in 1987 as London City Airport. There is little doubt that without the enthusiasm and determination of the West Country airline, the docklands facility would never have become a reality. Sadly, its livery is no longer to be seen at the airport, neither is it to be found elsewhere. A number of reorganisations resulted in the company being wholly owned by British Airways in August 1993, so the fleet now displays the colours of the flag carrier when flying on the network of regional routes.

FLEET:

DHC-7-110 Dash Seven: G-BRYA, G-BRYD
DHC-8-311 Dash Eight: G-BRYI, G-BRYJ, G-BRYK, G-BRYM, G-BRYO, G-BRYP, G-BRYR

UK airports served: Aberdeen, Bristol, Edinburgh, Glasgow, Guernsey, Heathrow, Jersey, Newquay, Newcastle, Plymouth, Southampton and Sumburgh.

Business Air — United Kingdom
Kirkhill Business House, Howemoss Drive, Dyce, Aberdeen — Tel: (01224) 725566

Established in 1987, Business Air has steadily grown in the past few years and now links a number of centres with regular services provided by its SAAB 340s. Most of these have been provided by the Swiss regional carrier, Crossair, which, together with Lufthansa, has a significant shareholding in the airline. Business Air started a schedule between London City and Frankfurt in 1993, but this has now been taken over by Lufthansa, albeit using the same BAe 146. Meanwhile, the Scottish company has launched several routes in competition with the

Above: **G-GNTA — SAAB SF340A of Business Air.**

larger carriers, including Manchester to Glasgow and Belfast, but the latter was discontinued in March 1996. Business Air became a member of the Airlines of Britain Group at the same time although its identity is retained. Neither Crossair nor Lufthansa now have a financial interest in the airline.

FLEET:
BAe 146-200: G-GNTZ
SAAB SF340A: G-GNTA, G-GNTB, G-GNTC, G-GNTD, G-GNTE, G-GNTF, G-GNTG
SAAB SF340B: G-, G-

UK airports served: Aberdeen, Dundee, East Midlands, Edinburgh, Glasgow, Inverness, Manchester and Sumburgh.

BWIA International (BW/BWA)　　　　Trinidad & Tobago
Administration Building, Piarco Airport, Trinidad　Tel: (809) 669 30

After British West Indian Airways was launched in 1939, its role was to provide links between Trinidad, Tobago and Barbados using a single Lockheed Lodestar. The airline became a subsidiary of British South American Airways (BSAA) in 1947, at which point the name British International Airways was adopted. Unfortunately, this phase was short-lived, so with the end of BSAA the company was obliged to revert to its BWIA identity. British Overseas Airways took over in 1949, but with no interference with the carrier's name. From 1961 the company became government controlled, by which time international services were being operated to North and South America and Europe in addition to the local commitments. The latter became the responsibility of Trinidad & Tobago Air Services in 1974, but after six years the pair were merged to produce greater efficiency.

Most of the schedules cover the Caribbean area with other sectors offered to the North American gateways of Miami, New York and Toronto. London remains a popular destination, which is not really surprising bearing in mind the number of visitors to the UK from the Caribbean. In early 1995 plans were well advanced for the privatisation of the airline, a process duly completed on 23 February. The Trinidad & Tobago government handed over 51% control to a group of private investors headed by Ed Acker, the one-time head of Air Florida and Pan Am. Future plans involve re-equipping the fleet with Boeing 757s and 767s although further reorganisation, including the departure of Acker, has delayed the decision. Airbus types may now be selected.

FLEET:

L1011-385 TriStar 500: 9Y-TGJ, 9Y-TGN, 9Y-THA, N3140, CS-TEA

Also operated are seven MD83s.

UK airport served: Heathrow.

Caledonian Airways (KT/CKT)   United Kingdom
Caledonian House, Gatwick Airport,
Crawley, West Sussex   Tel: (01293) 668280

The airline took over the combined charter activities of British Airtours and British Caledonian from 1 April 1988, at this point it became a wholly-owned subsidiary of British Airways. The airline provides IT charter flights for a number of independent tour operators, many of which are long-haul services to the Caribbean. In December 1994 Caledonian was bought by Inspirations in a deal which included five TriStars and the use of some 757s and DC-10s in order to fulfil the outstanding contracts held by the airline. Three Airbus A320s previously ordered by the new owner joined the fleet in time for the summer programme.

Below: **G-BBAJ — L1011-385 TriStar 100 of Caledonian Airways.**

FLEET:

Airbus A320-231: G-BVYA, G-BVYB, G-BVYC
Douglas DC-10-30: G-GOKT, G-NIUK
L1011-385 TriStar 1: G-BBAI
L1011-385 TriStar 50: G-CEAP
L1000-385 TriStar 100: G-BBAE, G-BBAF, G-BBAH, G-BBAJ

UK airports served: Birmingham, Gatwick, Glasgow, Luton and Manchester.

Canada 3000 Airlines (2T/CMM)   Canada
27 Fasken Drive, Toronto   Tel: (416) 674 02 57

When the airline began operations in 1988 it was known as Air 2000 Airlines but a name change became necessary at an early stage. Charters are flown to a large number of North American destinations from the major Canadian cities, while services are also operated to a number of points in the UK, together with other major European centres. The company retains its ties with the UK airline Air 2000 which includes the transfer of aircraft at off-peak occasions.

FLEET:

Airbus A320-212: C-GVXA, C-GVXB, C-GVXC, C-GVXD
Boeing 757-23A: C-FOOG, C-FXOK
Boeing 757-28A: C-FOOB, C-FOOE, C-FXOC, C-FXOF
Boeing 757-2Q8: C-FXOO

UK airports served: Birmingham, East Midlands, Gatwick, Glasgow and Manchester.

Canadian Airlines International (CP/CDN)   Canada
Scotia Centre 2800, 700-2nd Street SW, Calgary, Alberta   Tel: (403) 294 20 00

Canadian Pacific Airlines was created by the amalgamation of 10 small local carriers in 1942, with its activities confined mainly to the western and northwestern regions of the country. By 1949 the airline had received authority to introduce international services, the first to be launched being to Australia, Japan and Hong Kong, with others to New Zealand, Holland and Mexico inaugurated at intervals until 1955. In that year a bout of route swapping was carried out with Air Canada which gave CPA the traffic rights for the Toronto–Mexico City link in exchange for several domestic sectors in Ontario and Quebec.

In 1968 the company shortened its name to CP Air and had become Canada's second largest airline. Domestic trunk services were offered from all the major cities, while both transpacific and transatlantic schedules were flown. There was another name change in 1983 when the airline reverted to its original title, but five years later yet another identity was adopted when it merged with Pacific Western and BC Air Lines. The resultant carrier became Canadian International which nowadays visits 125 destinations worldwide.

FLEET:

Boeing 747-475: C-FBCA, C-FCRA, C-GMWW

Boeing 747-4F6: C-FGHZ

Boeing 767-375ER: C-FCAB, C-FCAE, C-FCAF, C-FCAG, C-FCAJ, C-FCAU, C-FOCA, C-FPCA, C-FTCA, C-FXCA, C-GLCA

Douglas DC-10-30: C-FCRD, C-FCRE, C-GCPC, C-GCPD, C-GCPE, C-GCPF, C-GCPG, C-GCPH, C-GCPI, C-GCPJ

Also operated are Airbus A320s and Boeing 737-200s.

UK airport served: Heathrow.

Cargolux (CV/CLX)   Luxembourg
Findel Airport, Luxembourg L-2900   Tel: 42 11 11

Cargolux was formed in 1970 with the help of Flugleidir Icelandair, Luxair and the Salen Shipping Co of Sweden. It is now Europe's largest cargo airline, with regular flights to Canada, the Near and Middle East, the Far East and the USA. Cargo charter flights are also arranged when required.

FLEET:

Boeing 747-271C: LX-ACV, LX-BCV, LX-ECV

Boeing 747-4R7F: LX-FCV, LX-GCV, LX-

UK airports served: None regularly.

Cathay Pacific Airways (CX/CPA)   Hong Kong
Swire House, 9 Connaught Road, Hong Kong   Tel: 747 50 50

At the end of World War 2, two airlines were formed in Hong Kong, one being Cathay Pacific Airways in 1946. To avoid any duplication of effort with Hong Kong Airways, Cathay applied itself to routes to the south, gradually changing from its charter role to an operator of scheduled services. By May 1953 these had reached Singapore, Bangkok, Saigon, Rangoon and Calcutta, but despite the success of the two carriers, it was decided that they should merge. This was completed in June 1959 with the pair coming under the Cathay Pacific title. Jet equipment was introduced in 1962 when a Convair 880 flew its first service on 8 April. Boeing 707s joined the company in 1971, while the first examples of the TriStar and Boeing 747 arrived in 1975 and 1979 respectively. Both types have continued to serve the airline, but the former is being phased out in favour of the Airbus A330 and A340. The larger 747-400 has also been introduced on to the carrier's worldwide schedules.

FLEET:

Airbus A340-313: VR-HXA, VR-HXB, VR-HXC, VR-HXD, VR-HXE, VR-HXF

Boeing 747-236F: VR-HVY

Boeing 747-267B: VR-HIA, VR-HIB, VR-HIC, VR-HID, VR-HIE, VR-HIF, VR-HKG

Boeing 747-267F: VR-HIH, VR-HVX, VR-HVZ

Boeing 747-367: VR-HII, VR-HIJ, VR-HIK, VR-HOL, VR-HOM, VR-HON

Boeing 747-467: VR-HOO, VR-HOP, VR-VOR, VR-HOS, VR-HOT, VR-HOU, VR-HOV, VR-HOW, VR-HOX, VR-HOY, VR-HOZ, VR-HUA, VR-HUB, VR-HUD, VR-HUE, VR-HUF, VR-HUG, VR-HUI, VR-HUJ

Boeing 747-467F: VR-HUH

Also operated are Airbus A330 and Boeing 777.

UK airports served: Heathrow and Manchester.

Centennial Airlines   Spain
Son Garcias Del Pinar, Coll d'En Rabassa,
E-07007 Palma   Tel: (71) 42 76 00

The airline began operations in February 1994 using a pair of MD83s for its planned scheduled service network. At the launch it was announced that four Airbus A320s were to be acquired as the carrier expanded, but in the event more MD83s joined the fleet. However, reservations have been made for two examples of the former for lease in 1996.

FLEET:

Airbus A320-231: EC-, EC-

McD Douglas MD83: EC-FSZ, EC-FVV, EC-GBV, EC-GFJ, EC-

UK airport served: Gatwick.

Channel Express (LS/EXS)   United Kingdom
Building 470, Bournemouth International Airport   Tel: (01202) 593344

Above; **G-STVN — HPR-7 Herald of Channel Express.**

From the time of its launch in January 1978 until 1982 the airline traded as Express Air Services. In that period both passenger and cargo work was carried out with a small fleet of Heralds, but gradually, as Channel Express, the carriage of freight between the Channel Islands and Bournemouth became the airline's main activity. While this link with Bournemouth is still maintained, general charters are nowadays operated throughout Europe, with the longer sectors flown by Electras. At night the fleet is busy with the movement of mail, small parcels and newspapers to and from a number of UK airports. Channel's Herald fleet has been expanded considerably through the years, with the aircraft brought up to modern standards with a much extended life expectancy.

FLEET:

Airbus A300B4: G-CEXC
F27 Friendship 500: G-CEXA, G-CEXB
F27 Friendship 600: G-BNIZ, G-CHNL
HPR-7 Herald: G-ASVO, G-AVPN, G-BEYF, G-CEAS, G-GNSY, G-SCTT, G-STVN
L188CF Electra: G-CEXS, G-CHNX, G-OFRT, N341HA, N343HA, N344HA

UK airports served: Bournemouth, Bristol, Cardiff, Coventry, East Midlands, Edinburgh, Exeter, Gatwick, Guernsey, Jersey, Liverpool, Newcastle and Stansted.

CityFlyer Express (FD/CFE)   United Kingdom
Iain Stewart Centre, Beehive Ring Road, Gatwick   Tel: (01293) 567837

Above: G-BVED — Aérospatiale ATR42-300 of CityFlyer Express/British Airways.

The airline was created after the collapse of Air Europe in 1991, initially taking the name Euroworld. This was changed to the present title in February 1992, while in April of that year the company became the first UK operator of the ATR42. As more of the type were received, so the original Short 360s were phased out, although the type remained in service until mid-1995. Since August

1993, CityFlyer has been operating successfully as a British Airways Express member, following the signing of a franchise agreement with the flag carrier. The first of two ATR72s was introduced in 1994, with the airline once again becoming the first UK carrier to operate the type.

FLEET:

Aérospatiale ATR42-300: G-BUEA, G-BUEB, G-BVEC, G-BVED, G-BVEF, G-BXEG, G-BXEH

Aérospatiale ATR72-202: G-BVTJ, G-BVTK, G-BVTL, G-BVTM

Avro RJ100: G-, G-

UK airports served: Birmingham, Gatwick, Guernsey, Jersey, Leeds/Bradford, Newcastle, Southend and Teesside.

CityJet (WX/BCY) — Eire
The Mezzanine, Terminal Building, Dublin   Tel: (1) 844 55 88

The Irish carrier began operations in early 1994 to provide regular links between Dublin and London City. The company was given the franchise for the services by Virgin Atlantic, but this ended in 1996 with the services now operated by CityJet on its own behalf.

FLEET:

BAe 146-200: EI-CMS, EI-CMY, EI-CNB

UK airports served: Jersey and London City.

Community Express Airlines (5V/UNI) — United Kingdom
Elmdon Building,
Birmingham International Airport B26 3QJ   Tel: (0121) 782 2747

Community Express was founded on 29 July 1993, but it was October 1995 before operations began with scheduled services linking East Midlands and Birmingham with Gatwick. A pair of Short SD3-60s were acquired from Mesa Air, but registration formalities obliged the airline to charter alternative equipment initially. A Jetstream 31 was leased on a short term basis from Maersk in early 1996 until the permanent machine completed its refurbishment. A second specimen was expected to join the carrier during the summer. In the meantime the two original 3-60s left the fleet to be replaced by another pair of the same breed, but this time leased from Jersey European/BAC Express. The airline's route network was also changed in the light of experience by adding Liverpool to the Birmingham-Gatwick link. Operations ceased at the end of September when the company entered administrative receivership.

FLEET:

BAe Jetstream 31: G-BRGN, G-BSIW

Short SD3-60: G-OBOH, G-

UK airports served: Belfast, Birmingham, Gatwick and Liverpool.

Condor Flugdienst (DE/CFG)   Germany
Postfach 1164, Langer Kornweg 32,
Kelsterbach D-65440   Tel: (6107) 93 90

This carrier was formed in October 1961, the result of a merger between
Deutsche Flugdienst and Condor Luftreederei, both being Lufthansa
subsidiaries. A modernisation programme was begun with the parent company
transferring four Viscounts to Condor, thereby greatly improving the
equipment then available to the German travel industry. Although a few
scheduled services were started, these were quickly dropped in order to
concentrate on the charter business. The airline soon began to expand into jet
operation with Boeing 727s, while longer range work became possible when
Lufthansa transferred some 707s in 1967.

Condor had the distinction of becoming the first charter airline to operate a
Boeing 747 configured with 500 seats when an example was delivered in 1971.
It was used to transport German tourists in bulk far afield until the late 1970s,
but falling demand necessitated the aircraft's disposal and it was replaced by
the slightly smaller DC-10. Throughout the 1980s Condor steadily expanded,
with the Boeing 757 becoming the mainstay of the fleet in the 1990s,
supported by 737s, 767s and a few DC-10s.

FLEET:

Boeing 737-35B: D-AGEC, D-AGED
Boeing 737-330: D-ABWA, D-ABWB
Boeing 757-27B: D-ABNX
Boeing 757-230: D-ABNA, D-ABNB, D-ABNC, D-ABND, D-ABNE, D-ABNF, D-ABNH, D-ABNI, D-ABNK, D-ABNL, D-ABNM, D-ABNN, D-ABNO, D-ABNP, D-ABNR, D-ABNS, D-ABNT
Boeing 767-330ER: D-ABUA, D-ABUB, D-ABUC, D-ABUD, D-ABUE, D-ABUF, D-ABUH, D-ABUI
Douglas DC-10-30: D-ADJO, D-ADLO, D-ADPO, D-ADQO, D-ADSO

UK airports served: None regularly.

Below: **D-ABNO — Boeing 757-230 of Condor Flugdienst.**

Continental Airlines (CO/COA)
2929 Allen Parkway, Houston Tx-77210

USA
Tel: (713) 834 50 00

Continental came into being in 1937 when the three-year-old Varney Speed Lines changed its name. In the early years the airline flew mainly local services, but in 1955 the award of a trunk route from Chicago to Los Angeles gave the carrier a start as a main line operator. In 1982 it was merged with Texas International which brought some rationalisation to the routes flown.

However, in September 1983 the airline was forced to seek the sanctuary of the American bankruptcy law (Chapter 11) while its affairs were reorganised. The restart was made with a severely pruned route network which had shed some 50 airports from its coverage, but it meant that Continental was able to emerge from Chapter 11 protection in 1985. Two years later it absorbed PeoplExpress and its associate New York Air. Financial problems returned in 1990 bringing another spell under Chapter 11 conditions until May 1993. In the meantime the company cancelled a large order for Airbus products, but surprisingly ordered 92 Boeing aircraft immediately it was free of the bankruptcy threat. Subsequently Continental has entered into an alliance with Air France and also has a close relationship with Alitalia and Air Canada.

FLEET:

Boeing 747-143: N17011
Boeing 747-230B: N78019
Boeing 747-238B: N17025
Boeing 747-243B: N33021
Boeing 757-224: N12114, N13110, N14115, N17104, N17105, N33103
Douglas DC-10-30: N12061, N12064, N13066, N13067, N14062, N14063, N15069, N19072, N41068, N68060, N68065, N76073, N83071, N87070
Also operated are DC-9, MD82 and Boeing 727/737/757.
On order are Boeing 767 and 777.

UK airports served: Gatwick and Manchester.

Below: **N19072 — Douglas DC-10-30 of Continental Airlines.**

Corsair (SS/CRL) — France
24 Rue Saarinen, Silic 221, F-94528 Rungis Silic   Tel: (1) 49 79 49 80

Formed in 1981, the company continues to provide international charter services throughout Europe, North America and the Mediterranean holiday areas.

FLEET:

Boeing 737-2A1: F-GHXK

Boeing 737-4B3: F-GFUG, F-GFUH

Boeing 747-121: F-GIMJ, F-GKLJ

Boeing 747-128: F-BPVG

Boeing 747-206B: F-GLNA, F-GPJM

Boeing 747-312: F-GSUN

Boeing 747SP-44: F-GTOM

UK airports served: None regularly.

Croatia Airlines (OU/CTN) — Croatia
Zrinjevak 17, Zagreb 41000   Tel: (1) 66 00 66

When the company was formed in 1989 it was known as Zagel (Zagreb Airlines), but it changed to the present identity in 1990. During parts of 1991 and 1992 the disturbances in Yugoslavia grounded the airline, but with the re-establishment of Croatia the country's flag carrier began to expand by introducing scheduled services, many having previously been flown by JAT. Croatia Airlines now serves 32 destinations throughout Europe with 737s leased from Lufthansa.

FLEET:

Boeing 737-230: 9A-CTA, 9A-CTB, 9A-CTC, 9A-CTD, 9A-CTE

Also operated are ATR42s.

UK airports served: Gatwick, Heathrow and Manchester.

Crossair (LX/CRX) — Switzerland
Postfach, CH-4002 Basel   Tel: (61) 325 25 25

The leading Swiss regional airline, Crossair is a subsidiary of Swissair. A large network of domestic and international scheduled services has been built up through the years, in some cases having taken over the route from the parent. Crossair was a launch customer for the SAAB 340 and again, more recently, for the 2000. In March 1995 it was announced that Crossair was to take over all flights involving aircraft with a capacity of up to 100 seats, which subsequently produced an order for 12 Avro RJ100s with deliveries starting in September. As the newcomers arrived they replaced Swissair's Fokker 100s which were then transferred to British Aerospace for resale. Another of Swissair's subsidiaries, Balair CTA, was also affected since its charter operations and some aircraft were also added to Crossair's responsibilities.

FLEET:

Avro RJ85: HB-IXF, HB-IXG, HB-IXH, HB-IXK

Avro RJ100: HB-IXM, HB-IXN, HB-IXO, HB-IXP, HB-IXQ, HB-IXR, HB-IXS, HB-IXT, HB-IXU, HB-IXV, HB-IXW, HB-IXX

McD Douglas MD82: HB-INR, HB-INV, HB-IUG, HB-IUH

McD Douglas MD83: HB-INW, HB-INZ, HB-ISX, HB-ISZ

SAAB SF340A: HB-AHB

SAAB SF340B: HB-AKA, HB-AKB, HB-AKC, HB-AKD, HB-AKE, HB-AKF, HB-AKG, HB-AKH, HB-AKI, HB-AKK, HB-AKL, HB-AKM, HB-AKN, HB-AKO, HB-AKP

SAAB 2000: HB-IZA, HB-IZB, HB-IZC, HB-IZD, HB-IZE, HB-IZF, HB-IZG, HB-IZH, HB-IZI, HB-IZK, HB-IZL, HB-IZM, HB-IZN, HB-IZO, HB-IZP, HB-IZQ, HB-IZR, HB-IZS, HB-IZT, HB-IZU, HB-IZV, HB-IZW, HB-IZX, HB-IZY, HB-IZZ

UK airports served: Birmingham, Edinburgh, Guernsey, Heathrow, Jersey, London City and Manchester.

Above: **HB-IZK — Saab 2000 of Crossair.** *Crossair*

CSA Czech Airlines (OK/CSA) — Czech Republic
Ruzyne Airport, CZ-16008 Praha 6 — Tel: (2) 36 89 21

One of Europe's oldest airlines, CSA can trace its origins back to 1923 when a state air transport group was formed. The airline began by operating a scheduled service between Prague and Bratislava, using a fleet of ex-military aircraft. Others were added during the 1920s, most of them linking cities within Czechoslovakia. In 1930 CSA changed this by opening a route to Zagreb, later becoming the first airline to provide a scheduled service from Western Europe to Russia.

With the occupation of Czechoslovakia in 1938, the airline was grounded until the intruders were evicted. The carrier was re-formed in 1945 by finding three tired Junkers Ju52s and some DC-3s to form a fleet. These were soon replaced by IL-12s, which in turn were succeeded by IL-14s. The Russian

Above: **OK-XGA — Boeing 737-555 of CSA Czech Airlines.**

influence continued with the airline's jet equipment for many years, but following the political developments in the 1980s, CSA turned to the west for its new aircraft.

Nowadays services are operated from Prague to most European centres, the Middle, Near and Far East, Africa and North and Central America. Domestic links have not been overlooked, with most of the major cities linked. In March 1995, the airline formally changed its name from Ceskoslovenske Aerolinie to CSA Czech Airlines.

FLEET:

Aérospatiale ATR72-202:	OK-XFA, OK-XFB, OK-XFC, OK-XFD, OK-XFE, OK-XFF
Airbus A310-304:	OK-WAA, OK-WAB
Boeing 737-4Y0:	OK-WGF, OK-WGG
Boeing 737-55S:	OK-XGA, OK-XGB, OK-XGC, OK-XGD, OK-XGE
Tupolev Tu-134A:	OK-EFJ, OK-EFK, OK-HFL, OK-HFM, OK-IFN
Tupolev Tu-154M:	OK-TCD, OK-UCE, OK-UCF, OK-VCG

UK airports served: Heathrow, Manchester and Stansted.

Cyprus Airways (CY/CYP)   Cyprus
PO Box 1903, 21 Alkeou Street, Nicosia   Tel: (2) 44 30 54

Cyprus Airways was formed in 1947 with a large interest held by British European Airways. The latter provided the services at first, but gradually the carrier began to operate its own regional services with DC-3s. Its activities were halted in 1955 due to unrest in the country, so BEA resumed the responsibility for all services. Eventually the local carrier restarted by leasing Viscounts to serve the Lebanon, Egypt and Israel.

Cyprus Airways acquired its first jet aircraft in September 1969 when a Trident 2 took over the Nicosia–London sector. The arrival of more of the type enabled other routes to benefit from the new equipment, that to Manchester becoming one such recipient. Unfortunately, in 1974 the relative calm was shattered by the unwelcome attentions of Turkish forces. During the ensuing invasion there was scant regard for civilian airliners, a lack of respect which accelerated Trident 5B-DAB's journey to the scrapyard. While the war raged, all operations were prudently suspended by Cyprus Airways; in fact it was seven months before two Viscounts leased from British Midland were able to resume some form of links between Larnaca, Athens, Beirut and Tel Aviv.

With some semblance of peace, the airline took delivery of One-Elevens and Boeing 707s for the longer routes, but one of the carrier's most ambitious steps was taken when Airbus A310s were ordered for delivery in 1984. The action provoked much local controversy, with allegations of inefficient management and the forecast of financial ruin both for the airline and the island, since by this time the government was the major shareholder. Needless to say, the carrier survived and indeed flourished. Its new equipment replaced the 707s on the London route and also took over some IT charter work. Later Cyprus Airways became one of the first customers for the A320.

FLEET:

Airbus A310-203: 5B-DAQ, 5B-DAR, 5B-DAS	
Airbus A310-204: 5B-DAX	
Airbus A320-231: 5B-DAT, 5B-DAU, 5B-DAV, 5B-DAW, 5B-DBA	

UK airports served: Birmingham, Gatwick, Heathrow, Manchester and Stansted.

Debonair Airways (2G/DEB)   United Kingdom
146 Prospect Way, London Luton Airport   Tel: (0541) 500146

Above: **G-DEBC — BAe 146-200 of Debonair.**

Founded as a low-cost, high-quality airline to provide a series of European scheduled services, the airline chose Luton as its first hub and headquarters after deciding against Gatwick. The first of seven ex-USAir BAe 146s was handed over in April after refurbishment by Marshall Aerospace, whereupon route proving commenced. With two aircraft on strength, Debonair was able to launch its operations on 19 June 1996 with Munich, Barcelona and Dusseldorf Express as the first destinations. Further routes were added as additional capacity became available, one of these being a domestic sector to Newcastle. The carrier intends to create at least one hub in Europe with direct links between points on the mainland, Munich-Barcelona being the first. British World's operator's certificate was used initially by Debonair pending the receipt of its own from the CAA.

FLEET:

BAe 146-200: G-DEBA, G-DEBC, G-DEBD, G-DEBE, G-DEBF, G-DEBG, G-DEBH

UK airports served: Luton and Newcastle.

Delta Air Lines (DL/DAL) — USA
Hartfield International Airport, Atlanta, Georgia 30320
Tel: (404) 715 26 00

In 1925 the Huff Daland Dusters began its service to agriculture by providing the world's first crop-spraying enterprise. The company branched out in 1929 to start passenger services between Dallas and Jackson, Mississippi, at the same time adopting a name more suited to the Mississippi Delta area it served. Progress was slow in the 1930s and even in 1942 Delta operated only nine airliners over its small network. This year marked a turning point in the carrier's fortunes because not only was New Orleans added to the coverage, but a licence was granted to include Miami. Larger aircraft were introduced in greater numbers which provided the impetus for further expansion in competition with Eastern, one of the established giants of the day. A number of mergers brought a wider area to develop, but it was the take-over of Northeast Airlines in 1972 that made Delta a force to be reckoned with throughout the United States. Apart from its vast domestic network, much of which radiates from the carrier's main hub at Atlanta, Delta nowadays operates internationally on the transatlantic routes to a number of European destinations, Canada, Central America and the Far East.

FLEET:

Boeing 767-332ER:	N171DN, N172DN, N173DN, N174DN, N175DN, N176DN, N177DN, N178DN, N179DN, N180DN, N181DN, N182DN, N183DN, N184DN, N185DN, N186DN, N187DN, N188DN, N189DN, N190DN, N191DN
L1011-385 TriStar 250:	N736DY, N737D, N740DA, N741DA, N1738D, N1739D
L1011-385 TriStar 500:	N751DA, N752DA, N753DA, N754DL, N755DL, N756DR, N759DA, N760DH, N761DA, N762DA, N763DL, N764DA, N765DA, N766DA, N767DA, N768DL, N769DL
McD Douglas MD11:	N801DE, N802DE, N803DE, N804DE, N805DE, N806DE, N807DE, N808DE, N809DE, N810DE, N811DE, N812DE, N813DE, N814DE, N815DE

Also operated are Boeing 727, 737, 757, 767-200, MD88, MD90 (on order) and TriStar 1.

UK airports served: Gatwick and Manchester.

Delta Air Transport (DAT)
Antwerp Airport, PO Box 4, B-2100 Deurne

Belgium
Tel: (3) 285 18 11

As is often the case, DAT began its career in 1966 by offering air-taxi and charter facilities, the DC-3 becoming the mainstay of the fleet until the type's withdrawal in 1972. Convair 440s and DC-6s were employed in the 1970s until these gave way to a fleet of Fairchild-Hiller FH-227Bs in 1977. The airline is a subsidiary of SABENA and operates various scheduled services for the flag carrier.

FLEET:

Avro RJ85: OO-DJK, OO-DJL, OO-DJN, OO-DJO, OO-DJP, OO-DJQ, OO-DJR, OO-DJS

BAe 146-200: OO-DJC, OO-DJD, OO-DJE, OO-DJF, OO-DJG, OO-DJH, OO-DJJ, OO-MJE

DHC-8-311 Dash Eight: PH-SDI, PH-SDJ, PH-SDM, PH-SDP, PH-SDR

EMB-120ER Brasilia: OO-DTF, OO-DTG, OO-DTH, OO-DTI, OO-DTJ, OO-DTL, OO-DTN, OO-DTO, OO-MTD

F28 Fellowship 1000: F-GBBR

F28 Fellowship 4000: OO-DJB

UK airports served: Bristol, Edinburgh, Glasgow, Heathrow, Leeds/Bradford, London City and Newcastle.

Denim Air (2D/DNM)
Luchthavenweg 15D, NL-5657 EA Eindhoven

Netherlands
Tel: (40) 257 08 73

The Dutch newcomer began operations on 26 April 1996 using a Fokker 50 to link its Eindhoven base with London City twice every weekday. As the name suggests, informality is intended and achieved by the use of denim for the aircrews' uniforms.

FLEET:

Fokker 50: PH-DMB, PH-DMO

UK airport served: London City.

Below: **PH-DMB — Fokker 50 of Denim Air.**

Deutsche BA (DI/BAG)　　　Germany
Wartungsallee 13, D-85356 Flughaven München　　Tel: (89) 97 59 15 00

The airline was formed in 1978 as Delta Air, thereafter operating regional scheduled services. However, in March 1993 ownership of the company was transferred to three German banks which took a 51% interest, with the remaining 49% going to British Airways. In the meantime the airline had adopted the present name.

FLEET:

Boeing 737-3L9: D-ADBA, D-ADBB, D-ADBC, D-ADBD, D-ADBE, D-ADBF, D-ADBG, D-ADBH, D-ADBI

Fokker 100: D-ADFA, D-ADFB, D-ADFC, D-ADFD, D-ADFE

SAAB 2000: D-ADSA, D-ADSB, D-ADSC, D-ADSD, D-ADSE

UK airports served: Gatwick, Guernsey and Jersey.

DHL Worldwide Express (DHL/BCS)　　USA
PO Box 75122, Cincinnati, Ohio 45275　　Tel: (606) 283 22 32

This express parcel and courier airline was establsihed in 1969 to link Hawaii with San Francisco, but has subsequently created 12 hubs and 76 gateways worldwide. In addition to its own aircraft, those of other contracted carriers also carry DHL's livery and titles.

FLEET:

Douglas DC-8-73F: N801DH, N802DH, N803DH, N804DH, N805DH, N806DH, N807DH

Convair 580s and Boeing 727s of European Air Transport fly in full DHL livery.

UK airports served: Aberdeen, Coventry, East Midlands, Edinburgh, Glasgow, Heathrow, Luton and Stansted.

easyJet Airline (EZY)　　United Kingdom
Easyland, London Luton International　　Tel: (01582) 445566

Formed in October 1995 by the owners of a Greek shipping line, the carrier began operations one month later with a domestic route between its Luton hub and Glasgow. This was soon followed by Edinburgh and Aberdeen, while Amsterdam became easyJet's first international sector in the spring of 1996. The airline offers low fares which are made possible by the no-frills policy with direct-sell rather than using travel agents for reservations.

FLEET:

Boeing 737-204: G-BECG, G-BECH

Boeing 737-3Y0: G-EZYA, G-

UK airports served: Aberdeen, Edinburgh, Glasgow and Luton.

Edelweiss Air (EDW)　　　　　Switzerland
Postfach, CH-8058 Zurich-Flughafen　　　Tel: (1) 816 50 60

The airline was set up by a former executive of Balair/CTA to provide low-cost flights from Switzerland to a variety of destinations. This includes the UK, with regular visits now made to Luton by the carrier's ex-Airtours MD83s.

FLEET:

McD Douglas MD83: HB-IKM, HB-IKN

UK airports served: Luton and others for charter work.

EgyptAir (MS/MSR)　　　　　　Egypt
Cairo International Airport, Heliopolis　　　Tel: (2) 390 24 44

The Egyptian flag carrier took the name EgyptAir on 10 October 1971, although its origins go back to 1932. Other identities used through the years include Misr Airwork, Misrair and United Arab Airlines. At first services were on a fairly modest scale, but an international route was inaugurated in 1933 linking Cairo with Haifa and later Baghdad. The airline's commercial activities were taken over by the government in 1939, but it was another 10 years before the carrier became wholly Egyptian owned. At this stage Vikings were employed, a type replaced by French Languedocs for a short spell before the airline became one of the first Middle East operators of the new turboprop Viscount in 1955. During 1956 the company's fleet was reduced in size when it unwillingly became involved in the Suez affray. Many of its possessions were reduced to scrap value during this short interlude, but surprisingly re-equipment plans included an order for the Comet.

Below: SU-GBG — Airbus A320-231 of EgyptAir.

FLEET:

Airbus A300-622R: SU-GAR, SU-GAS, SU-GAT, SU-GAU, SU-GAV, SU-GAW, SU-GAX, SU-GAY, SU-GAZ

Airbus A320-231: SU-GBA, SU-GBB, SU-GBC, SU-GBD, SU-GBE, SU-GBF, SU-GBG

Boeing 747-366: SU-GAL, SU-GAM

Boeing 767-266ER: SU-GAH, SU-GAI, SU-GAJ

Boeing 767-366ER: SU-GAO, SU-GAP

Boeing 777-266: SU-GBP, SU-GBR, SU-GBS

UK airports served: Heathrow and Manchester.

El Al Israel Airlines (LY/ELY) — Israel
PO Box 41, Ben Gurion International Airport 70100 — Tel: (3) 971 61 11

Above: **4X-EBV — Boeing 757-258 of El Al.**

In 1948 there was an Israeli/Arab disagreement raging. This was not an unknown event in that period, but during the year a compromise was found, thereby bringing an end to the unpleasantness. It did not last, of course, but the Israelis found time to form a national carrier which took the name El Al. International services were begun in August 1949 and in due course the airline became the first outside Europe and America to operate transatlantic schedules. El Al later re-equipped with the Britannia, becoming the second customer to buy the machine for its long-haul work. The aircraft's reign did not last long, because the type was overtaken by progress and replaced on the New York run by Boeing 707s in May 1961.

As the years advanced, so El Al's problems have increased. When on the ground its aircraft are under strict security control, while checks of passengers' belongings are more thorough than most. Financial troubles have caused a number of temporary setbacks such as a four-month suspension of activity in 1982. Yet another difficulty has been created by the government banning Saturday movements, the day of the Jewish Sabbath. Despite all these handicaps, El Al manages to maintain services to North America, Europe and Africa.

FLEET:

Boeing 747-124F: 4X-AXZ	
Boeing 747-238B: 4X-AXQ	
Boeing 747-245F: 4X-AXK, 4X-AXL	
Boeing 747-258B: 4X-AXA, 4X-AXB, 4X-AXC, 4X-AXH, 4X-AXQ	
Boeing 747-258C: 4X-AXD, 4X-AXF	
Boeing 747-458: 4X-ELA, 4X-ELB, 4X-ELC	
Boeing 757-258: 4X-EBL, 4X-EBM, 4X-EBR, 4X-EBS, 4X-EBT, 4X-EBU, 4X-EBV	
Boeing 757-27B: 4X-EBF	
Boeing 767-258: 4X-EAA, 4X-EAB	
Boeing 767-258ER: 4X-EAC, 4X-EAD	

UK airports served: Heathrow and Manchester.

Emerald Airways (JEM) — United Kingdom
South Terminal, Speke Hall Avenue, Liverpool — Tel: (0151) 448 0844

When formed in December 1987, the airline was known as Janes Aviation, with its base at Blackpool. It began cargo charters from this airport during 1988 with a DC-3, but this was later replaced by a number of HS748s. A move to Liverpool followed, from where both passenger and freight charters are flown. Contracts are also held for the movement of parcels and mail on behalf of the Post Office. The airline plans to operate scheduled passenger services, the first likely to be Liverpool-Isle of Man.

FLEET:

Avro 748 Srs 1: G-BEJD, G-BEJE, G-DAAL
HS748 Srs 2A: G-ATMI, G-ATMJ, G-AYIM, G-BGMO, G-BIUV, G-BPDA, G-BVOU, G-BVOV
HS748 Srs 2B: G-HDBD, G-OJEM

UK airports served: Belfast, Coventry, Edinburgh, Isle of Man, Leeds/Bradford, Liverpool and Stansted.

Emirates (EK/UAE) — United Arab Emirates
PO Box 686, Dubai — Tel: (4) 82 25 11

Wholly owned by the government of Dubai, the airline was established in 1985 to operate a worldwide network of scheduled services. Subsequently, Emirates has concentrated its coverage on Europe and the Middle and Far East, with no transatlantic sorties at present. With the exception of two Boeing 727s, the airline's fleet is comprised of Airbus products, although this will change in 1996 when deliveries of its Boeing 777s begin.

FLEET:

Airbus A300-605R: A6-EKC, A6-EKD, A6-EKE, A6-EKF, A6-EKM, A6-EKO

Airbus A310-304: A6-EKA, A6-EKB, A6-EKG, A6-EKN

Airbus A310-308: A6-EKH, A6-EKI, A6-EKJ, A6-EKK, A6-EKL, A6-EKP

Boeing 777-21H: A6-EMD, A6-EME, A6-EMF, A6-EMG, A6-EMH, A6-EMI, A6-EMJ

UK airports served: Heathrow and Manchester.

Estonian Air (OV/ELL) — Estonia
Vabaduse Valjak 10, Tallinn — Tel: (2) 44 63 83

Estonia was one of the early countries to break away from the control of the Soviet Union, with the result that Estonian Air was created in 1991. Until 1995 the airline was obliged to use its inefficient ex-Aeroflot aircraft, many of which have now been retired. The airline decided to replace all its aircraft with Western-built types, so two Boeing 737-500s were acquired to take over the scheduled service duties.

FLEET:

Boeing 737-5Q8: ES-ABC, ES-ABD

Tupolev Tu-154A: ES-AAE, ES-AAH, ES-AAL, ES-AAN

UK airport served: Gatwick.

Ethiopian Airlines (ET/ETH) — Ethiopia
PO Box 1755, Addis Ababa — Tel: (1) 61 22 22

Ethiopia formed its national carrier in December 1945 in readiness for the start of scheduled services on 8 April 1946. Not surprisingly, DC-3s formed the fleet which was used for domestic links. Later, as more suitable equipment was obtained, international schedules were offered. Nowadays Ethiopian visits numerous destinations in Africa, while Europe and the Middle and Far East also feature in the route network.

FLEET:

Boeing 757-260: ET-AJS, ET-AJX, ET-AKC, ET-AKE, ET-AKF

Boeing 767-260ER: ET-AIE, ET-AIF, ET-AIZ

UK airport served: Heathrow.

Euralair International (RN/EUL)   France
Aéroport Le Bourget, F-93350 Le Bourget, Paris   Tel: (1) 49 34 62 00

Air-taxi work was the first activity for Euralair after it was formed in October 1964. Although the airline subsequently operated both charter and scheduled passenger services for many years, in 1995 it transferred the latter operations to Air Liberté in order to concentrate on its charter commitments. Several Boeing 737s were included in the transaction. In addition, the carrier often operates aircraft for other airlines such as Air Charter and Air France.

FLEET:

Airbus A321-111: F-G, F-G	
Airbus A330-321: F-G, F-G	
Boeing 737-2A9C: F-GFYL	
Boeing 737-53A: F-GGML	
Boeing 737-53C: F-GHOL, F-GHUL, F-GINL	

UK airports served: None regularly, occasional charters only.

Euro Direct Belgium (SFI)   Belgium
Luchthavenstraat 1, Bus 14, B-8560 Wevelgem   Tel: (56) 37 01 21

Euro Direct stems from Skyfreighters which operated for Federal Express in the late 1980s from Brussels. When this work ended due to the cessation of the US company's European network, the Belgian airline operated a scheduled service between Kortrijk and Stansted with a Bandeirante which did not prove particularly successful. However, the route was restarted in October 1994 by joining the growing Euro Direct (UK)'s network, although the Belgian carrier remained independent. A Jetstream 31 was registered and transferred to the company by the UK airline, but at the end of February 1995 the latter ceased operations, to the surprise of its European associate. After obtaining more financial backing, Euro Direct Belgium was able to survive and launch a scheduled service between Brussels and Humberside on 3 April. It later became a SABENA route but still flown by the Jetstream.

FLEET:

BAe Jetstream 31: OO-EDA

UK airport served: Humberside.

EuroBelgian Airlines (BQ/EBA)   Belgium
Building 116, B-1820 Melsbroek Airport, Brussels   Tel: (2) 752 05 11

EuroBelgian Airlines was formed in November 1991 in the wake of the collapse of Trans European. It has since concentrated on charter work with its Boeing 737 fleet, but an entry has now been made into the scheduled scene. A majority interest in the airline was acquired by Virgin Atlantic in April 1996 to

Above: **OO-LTR — Boeing 737-4S3 of EBA EuroBelgian Airlines.** *A. S. Wright*

enable the UK carrier to create Virgin European Express. A number of routes will be flown from the Brussels hub.

FLEET:

Boeing 737-3M8: OO-LTJ, OO-LTL	
Boeing 737-3Y0: OO-LTV, OO-LTY, OO-VEA, OO-VEB	
Boeing 737-33A: OO-LTP, OO-LTU, OO-LTW	
Boeing 737-436: OO-LTQ, OO-LTS	
Boeing 737-4S3: OO-LTR	

UK airports served: Birmingham, Gatwick, Manchester and Stansted.

Eurocypria Airlines (UI/ECA)   Cyprus
97 Artemidos Avenue, Artemis Building,
PO Box 970, Larnaca   Tel: (4) 65 00 00

Below: **5B-DBC — Airbus A320-231 of Eurocypria Airways.** *A. S. Wright*

Cyprus Airways set up its wholly-owned subsidiary in 1991, with operations starting in March 1992. Charters have since been flown from Larnaca and Paphos to most European cities using three A320s leased from the parent company.

FLEET:

Airbus A320-231: 5B-DBB, 5B-DBC, 5B-DBD

UK airports served: Glasgow and Luton.

Eurofly (EEZ) — Italy

Aeroporto Citta di Torino,
I-10072 Caselle Torinese
Tel: (11) 470 44 44

This Turin-based carrier operates passenger charters to Europe, Africa and the Middle East. It was formed in May 1989 with two DC-9-51s. As a subsidiary of Alitalia, Eurofly also has access to MD80s as required.

FLEET:

Douglas DC-9-51: I-FLYY, I-FLYZ

McD Douglas MD83: EI-CEK, EI-CMM

UK airports served: None regularly.

European Air Transport (QY/BCS) — Belgium

Building 4-5, Brussels National Airport,
Zaventem B-1930
Tel: (2) 718 14 14

The airline was established in 1971 to operate regional passenger and cargo services from Brussels. Since being purchased by DHL Worldwide Express in 1986, the airline has become mainly occupied with the overnight movement of mail and small parcels. Sorties are made to a wide number of European airports by the large fleet of Boeing 727s and Convair 580s.

FLEET:

Boeing 727-31C: OO-DHM, OO-DHN, OO-DHO

Boeing 727-35F: OO-DHP, OO-DHQ, OO-DHR

Boeing 727-223F: OO-DHS, OO-DHT, OO-DHU, OO-DHV, OO-DHW, OO-DHX

Convair Cv580F: OO-DHC, OO-DHD, OO-DHE, OO-DHF, OO-HUB

UK airports served: Aberdeen, Coventry, East Midlands, Edinburgh, Heathrow, Luton and Stansted.

European Airways (L8/EAW) — United Kingdom

Newcastle International Airport
Tel: (0191) 214 4633

Operations finally began for this new carrier on 27 February 1995 when its Jetstream left Newcastle on a scheduled run to and from Southampton.

Uzbekistan Airways holds a 40% share in the company, so it is not surprising that the company has plans for a service to Tashkent. Nearer home, both Barcelona and Hamburg are being considered for future expansion. In the meantime an Exeter-Manchester service was planned.

FLEET:

BAe Jetstream 3102: G-CBEA, G-OBEA

UK airports served: Newcastle and Southampton.

European Aviation Air Charter (EAF)   United Kingdom
European House, Bournemouth International
Airport, Dorset   Tel: (01202) 581111

European Aviation Air Charter began operations in February 1994 following the purchase of an initial batch of One-Eleven 500s from British Airways. A further four were subsequently obtained from the same source. The aircraft are employed for IT charter work, *ad hoc* charters, scheduled services and leases to other carriers such as AB Shannon, Air Bristol and Ryanair. One of the One-Elevens (G-AZMF) is equipped with a 50-seat cabin for VIP work.

FLEET:

BAC One-Eleven 501EX: G-AWYV
BAC One-Eleven 510ED: G-AVMH, G-AVMI, G-AVMK, G-AVML, G-AVMM, G-AVMN, G-AVMP, G-AVMR, G-AVMS, G-AVMT, G-AVMV, G-AVMW, G-AVMX, G-AVMY, G-AVMZ
BAC One-Eleven 518FG: VR-BED
BAC One-Eleven 521FH: VR-BEC
BAC One-Eleven 523FJ: G-AXLL
BAC One-Eleven 524FF: VR-BEA, VR-BEB
BAC One-Eleven 530FX: G-AYOP, G-AZMF
Boeing 727-51: OK-TGX

UK airports served: Various as required for charters.

Below: **G-AVMI — BAC One-Eleven 510ED of European Aviation Air Charter.**

Eurowings (EW/EWG) — Germany
Flughafenstrasse 100, Nürnberg D-90411   Tel: (231) 92 45 101

This German regional airline was created through the 1992 merger of Dortmund-based RFG with Nuremberg-based NFD. In addition to domestic services, the carrier operates a number of international flights with its large ATR42 and 72 fleet.

FLEET:

Aérospatiale ATR42-300: D-BAAA, D-BBBB, D-BCCC, D-BCRM, D-BCRN, D-BCRO, D-BCRP, D-BCRQ, D-BCRR, D-BCRS, D-BCRT, D-BDDD, D-BEEE, D-BFFF, D-BGGG, D-BHHH, D-BJJJ

Aérospatiale ATR72-202: D-ANFA, D-ANFB, D-ANFC, D-ANFD, D-ANFE, D-ANFF

Aérospatiale ATR72-212: D-AEWG, D-AEWH, D-AEWI, D-AEWK, D-AEWL, D-A

Airbus A319-100: D-, D-, D-

BAe 146-200: D-ACFA, D-ADEI, D-AJET, D-ANTJ

BAe 146-300: D-AEWA, D-AEWB

Above: **D-ACFA — BAe 146-200 of Eurowings.** *A. S Wright*

UK airport served: Gatwick, Guernsey and Jersey.

EVA Airways (BR/EVA) — Taiwan
376 Hsin-nan Road, Luchu,
Taoyuan Hsien, Taiwan   Tel: (3) 351 51 51

The airline was formed in 1989 whereupon it began to order its new equipment to enable scheduled services to start in 1991. Initially the airline concentrated on Asian destinations, but as its fleet expanded, so it opened new routes to Europe and the US.

Boeing 747-45E: B-16401, B-16402, B-16461, B-16462, B-16463, B-16465,
 N403EV, N405EV, N406EV, N407EV, N408EV, N409EV

Also operated are Boeing 767s and MD11s

UK airport served: Heathrow.

Excalibur Airways (EXC)
Beverley Road, East Midlands Airport

United Kingdom
Tel: (01332) 850320

The airline was formed in 1992 from the assets of TEA (UK) which had ceased
trading following the collapse of the Belgian parent company. The airline
opted for a fleet of 180-seat Airbus A320s for its proposed IT charter work, a
type which has since become very popular with the passengers. Most of its
activities are centred upon Gatwick and Manchester, but flights are also
operated from several other regional airports. In November 1995 Excalibur was
purchased by the Scottish tour operator Globespan which accelerated the
carrier's change from short/medium-haul charters to long-haul with a pair of
DC-10s. Late deliveries led to sub-leasing aircraft to meet its commitments, but
a number of problems were experienced and the company was forced to end
all flying in mid-1996.

Federal Express (FM/FDX)
PO Box 727, Memphis International Airport, Tennessee 38194

USA
Tel: (901) 369 36 00

The company is now the world's largest express carrier with its main centre of
operations at Memphis. Since it began operations in 1973, FedEx has built up
an enormous network of nightly run services, especially for the movement of
small packets and parcels. The activities were confined to the US for some years,
but in 1985 the airline extended its coverage to Europe. Initially the
transatlantic trips were covered by some specially modified Boeing 727s, but as
loads increased, so DC-10s were introduced.

FLEET:
Boeing 747-245F: N636FE, N638FE, N640FE, N641FE

Below: N305FE — Douglas DC-10-30 of Federal Express.

Boeing 747-2R7F: N639FE

Douglas DC-10-30: N301FE, N302FE, N303FE, N304FE, N305FE, N306FE, N307FE, N308FE, N309FE, N310FE, N311FE, N312FE, N313FE, N314FE, N315FE, N316FE, N317FE, N318FE, N319FE, N320FE, N321FE, N322FE

McD Douglas MD11: N582FE, N583FE, N584FE, N586FE, N601FE, N602FE, N603FE, N604FE, N605FE, N606FE, N607FE, N608FE, N609FE, N610FE, N611FE, N612FE, N614FE, N615FE, N616FE, N617FE, N-, N-, N-

UK airports served: Prestwick and Stansted.

Finnair (AY/FIN)   Finland
Dagmarinkatu 4, FIN-00100 Vantaa   Tel: (0) 81 881

Operations began in 1924 with a scheduled service linking Helsinki, Tallinn and Stockholm. The company's ability to maintain the operation through a particularly bad winter in 1925/26 impressed the Finnish government to such an extent that it offered loans and subsidies to provide the means to acquire additional aircraft. Until 1936 these were exclusively seaplanes, but following the construction of some airfields, landplanes became a practical proposition. In common with most European countries, activities during World War 2 were severely affected. A few domestic flights were maintained, but it was 1947 before the first postwar link with Stockholm was introduced. With nine DC-3s on strength the network was gradually expanded, but the company's London inaugural did not come until 1954, with Moscow added two years later to give the Finnish carrier the distinction of being the only Western company to receive such permission at that time. Until 1968 the airline was known as Aero O/Y, but during the year this was changed to its present title, Finnair.

Above: **OH-LAA — Airbus A300B4-203 of Finnair.**

FLEET:

Airbus A300B4-203: OH-LAA, OH-LAB

Boeing 757-2Q8: OH-, OH-, OH-, OH-

Douglas DC-9-51: OH-LYN, OH-LYO, OH-LYP, OH-LYR, OH-LYS, OH-LYT,
OH-LYU, OH-LYV, OH-LYW, OH-LYX, OH-LYY, OH-LYZ

McD Douglas MD11: OH-LGA, OH-LGB, OH-LGC, OH-LGD

McD Douglas MD82: OH-LMH, OH-LMN, OH-LMO, OH-LMP, OH-LMT, OH-LMW,
OH-LMX, OH-LMY, OH-LMZ, OH-LPA

McD Douglas MD83: OH-LMG, OH-LMR, OH-LMS, OH-LMU, OH-LMV, OH-LPB,
OH-LPC, OH-LPD, OH-LPE, OH-LPH

McD Douglas MD87: OH-LMA, OH-LMB, OH-LMC

UK airports served: Gatwick, Glasgow, Heathrow, Manchester and Stansted.

Flightline (FLT) — United Kingdom
Aviation Way, Southend Airport — Tel: (01702) 543000

Above: **G-BPNT — BAe 146-300 of Palmair Flightline.**

Passenger charters are operated with two BAe 146s, one based at
Bournemouth to fly ITs on behalf of Palmair. The second, is used for Swiss
charters from a Stansted base. Freight work is also undertaken, using
Bandeirantes for this purpose.

FLEET:

BAe 146-200: G-OZRH

BAe 146-300: G-BPNT

EMB-110P1 Bandeirante: G-FLTY, G-OFLT

UK airports served: Aberdeen, Bournemouth, Bristol, Edinburgh, Guernsey,
Jersey, Southend and Stansted.

Fred Olsen (FO/FOF)   Norway
PO Box 10, N-1330 Oslo Lufthavn   Tel: (67) 53 09 00

Fred Olsen was already a leading Norwegian shipping company when the company began to expand into the air transport business in 1933. A considerable sum was invested in the national carrier Det Norske Luftfartelskap (DNL), thereby enabling domestic services to begin, followed by links with Amsterdam and Copenhagen. After the war, Fred Olsen became more involved in leasing, a pursuit which proved very successful. Nowadays much of the company's income is derived from regular freight services and the nightly movement of small parcels throughout Europe.

FLEET:

L188AF Electra: LN-FOG, LN-FOH, LN-FOI, LN-FOL, LN-FON, LN-FOO

UK airports served: None regularly.

Futura International Airways (FH/FUA)   Spain
Grand Via Asuma 17, E-07009 Palma   Tel: (71) 75 51 96

Above: EC-EVE — Boeing 737-4YO of Futura International Airways.

Futura was one of several Spanish charter companies that were set up with the help of other airlines to win a share of the country's IT market. In this case Aer Lingus has an 85% share in the airline which was established in 1990.

FLEET:

Boeing 737-4Y0: EC-ETB, EC-EVE, EC-EXY, EC-FLD, EC-FZT, EC-GHF, EC-GHK
Boeing 737-4S3: EC-GFE

UK airports served: Aberdeen, Belfast, Birmingham, Bristol, Cardiff, Exeter, Gatwick, Glasgow, Humberside, Liverpool, Manchester, Newcastle and Prestwick.

In the years before World War 2, KLM enjoyed considerable success in the East Indies with its subsidiary KNILM. The Japanese invasion encouraged a swift move of the airline's possessions to Australia for the duration, where they were used by the military. Although peace was officially restored to the area in 1945, a protracted outbreak of political skirmishes within Indonesia did not allow the Dutch-owned company much scope for survival. Finally a new airline was formed as Garuda Indonesian Airways, which was a joint venture by KLM and the government. However, it was not long before the carrier became wholly state owned and by 1956 all links with KLM had been severed.

The first international routes were opened in 1954 to reach Bangkok, Manila and Singapore, but since that time Garuda's coverage has been expanded to include Europe, the Middle East and Australia. The Indonesian flag carrier became the first operator in the world to put wide-bodied airliners into service with two crew members on the flightdeck, when its Airbus A300s began to arrive in January 1982.

FLEET:

Boeing 747-2U3B: PK-GSA, PK-GSB, PK-GSC, PK-GSD, PK-GSE, PK-GSF
Boeing 747-4U3: PK-GSG, PK-GSH
Boeing 747-441: PK-GSI
Douglas DC-10-30: PK-GIA, PK-GIB, PK-GIC, PK-GID, PK-GIE, PK-GIF
McD Douglas MD11: EI-CDI, EI-CDJ, EI-CDK, PK-GIG, PK-GII, PK-GIJ, PK-, PK-, PK-
Also operated are Airbus A300B4s and A300-622Rs, with A330-300s on order for delivery in 1996/97.

UK airport served: Gatwick.

The airline was formed in 1931, trading as Gibair until the early 1980s. A number of scheduled services to North African destinations are flown from Heathrow, while the company's base at Gatwick serves as the UK terminal for the Gibraltar and Madeira flights. An extensive IT charter programme is maintained, with the aircraft employed flying under the name GB Leisure. The airline has a franchise agreement with British Airways.

FLEET:

Boeing 737-236: G-BGDS, G-BGDU
Boeing 737-4Q8: G-BNNK, G-BNNL
Boeing 737-4S3: G-BUHL, G-TREN

UK airports served: Gatwick, Heathrow and Manchester.

Above: **D-AGEH — Boeing 737-3L9 of Germania.**

The carrier took the name Special Air Transport when it was formed in 1978 to operate charters to the Mediterranean area with Caravelles acquired from LTU. In due course the latter type was supplemented by a pair of Boeing 727s from Hapag Lloyd, the entire fleet later giving way to Boeing 737-300s. The airline changed its name to Germania in June 1986, but its charter activities still take its aircraft to all the usual holiday destinations. In March 1995 the carrier became a launch customer for the new Boeing 737-700, which will be configured with 148 seats when deliveries begin towards the end of 1997. Four 737s (D-ABWA/B and D-AGEC/D) are operated by Condor in the latter's full livery.

FLEET:

Boeing 737-35B: D-AGEA, D-AGEB, D-AGEC, D-AGED, D-AGEE, D-AGEF, D-AGEG

Boeing 737-3L9: D-AGEH, D-AGEI, D-AGEJ

Boeing 737-330: D-ABWA, D-ABWB

UK airports served: None regularly.

Ghana Airways (GH/GHA)   Ghana
PO Box 1636, Ghana House, Accra   Tel: (21) 77 75 88

Following the independence of the country hitherto known as the Gold Coast, the government of the newly-created Ghana formed a national carrier on 4 July 1958. Its role was to take over the services which related to that part of Africa, considerable assistance being given by BOAC. The latter held a 40% share in the company and was therefore willing to supply a Boeing Stratocruiser for the reinstated Accra–London route in July 1958. Domestic operations quickly followed and by the time that the British involvement ended in 1961, the airline was reasonably established. Nowadays Ghana Airways employs a DC-10 on its long-haul sectors, while regional and domestic services are handled by a DC-9 and a pair of Fellowships respectively.

FLEET:

Douglas DC-10-30: 9G-ANA

Also operated are two Fellowships and a DC-9.

UK airport served: Heathrow.

Gill Airways (9C/GIL) United Kingdom
Newcastle International Airport, Tyne & Wear Tel: (0191) 286 9665

Above: **G-BWDB — Aérospatiale ATR72-202 of Gill Airways.**

Through the years since its creation in 1969, the airline has progressed from air-taxi operations to scheduled services. The latter began in 1989 and now provide connections from Newcastle to a number of destinations in England, Scotland and Northern Ireland. The airline is also involved in the movement of personnel for the oil industry, while mail flights provide employment for the aircraft during the night.

FLEET:

Aérospatiale ATR42-300: G-BVJP, G-ORFH

Aérospatiale ATR72-202: G-BWDA, G-BWDB

Short SD3-60: G-BLGE, G-BLZT, G-BNFB, G-BVMX, G-DASI, G-OLAH, G-RMCT

UK airports served: Aberdeen, Belfast, Bournemouth, Bristol, Carlisle, East Midlands, Edinburgh, Gatwick, Humberside, Isle of Man, Leeds/Bradford, Liverpool, Manchester, Newcastle, Prestwick, Stansted and Wick.

Gulf Air (GF/GFA)   Gulf States
PO Box 138, Manama, Bahrain   Tel: 32 22 00

The carrier was established as Gulf Aviation in 1950, but for many years it confined its operations to regional services. In 1973 it was decided that a new image was desirable, so the name Gulf Air was adopted in readiness for the planned changes.

For some time BOAC VC10s had been used on the twice-weekly flights to London, but with the departure of the British from that part of the world in 1972, the opportunity was there for the airline to emerge as a leading operator in its own right. Ownership was split equally between the governments of Bahrain, Oman, Qatar and the United Arab Emirates on 1 April 1974, the same date marking the introduction of the airline's own VC10s on the trunk routes. Expansion plans were ambitious and expensive, but this was of little consequence since the money spent was more than covered by the constant flow of oil. Some of the funds no doubt paid for a few TriStars, the first arriving in January 1976. This type remained the mainstay of the fleet for some years, but in recent times both the Boeing 767 and Airbus A340 have taken over from the trijets.

FLEET:

Airbus A340-312: A4O-LA, A4O-LB, A4O-LC, A4O-LD, A4O-LE, A4O-LF

Boeing 767-3P6ER: A4O-GH, A4O-GI, A4O-GJ, A4O-GK, A4O-GL, A4O-GM, A4O-GN, A4O-GO, A4O-GP, A4O-GR, A4O-GS, A4O-GT, A4O-GU, A4O-GV, A4O-GW, A4O-GX, A4O-GY, A4O-GZ

Also operated are Airbus A320-212s.

UK airport served: Heathrow.

Hamburg Airlines (HX/HAS)   Germany
Flughaven Gebäude 175, Hamburg D-22335   Tel: (40) 5075 29 02

Formed in 1988, the carrier operates a number of regional and international scheduled services from its main base at Hamburg, while charter flights are also offered. Until the end of 1994 the airline employed only turboprops for all activities, but the BAe 146 has now been added for use on the busier routes.

FLEET:

BAe 146-200: D-ALOA, D-ASUR

BAe 146-300: D-AHOI

DHC-8-102 Dash Eight: D-BOBL, D-BOBO, D-BOBY

DHC-8-311 Dash Eight: D-BOBA, D-BOBU

UK airports served: None regularly.

Founded in July 1972 by the German shipping group of the same name, Hapag-Lloyd began its operations on 31 March 1973. Since that time, the airline has become one of Germany's leading charter carriers with services to all the European holiday destinations. In 1979 the company merged with its rival, Bavaria-Germanair, itself the result of an earlier take-over. Hapag-Lloyd was an operator of the Airbus A300 for some years and was the first to employ the series C4 convertible version in January 1980. Subsequently the A310 variant replaced the larger machines, while the mainstay of the fleet has become the Boeing 737-400 and 500, to which will be added the new 180-seat Series 800 when deliveries start in 1998. No doubt these will replace some of the earlier machines with the customary transfer of the D-AH registration sequence.

FLEET:

Airbus A310-204: D-AHLV, D-AHLW, D-AHLX, D-AHLZ

Airbus A310-304: D-AHLA, D-AHLB, D-APOM

Airbus A310-308: D-AHLC

Boeing 737-4K5: D-AHLG, D-AHLJ, D-AHLK, D-AHLL, D-AHLM, D-AHLO, D-AHLP, D-AHLQ, D-AHLR, D-AHLS, D-AHLT, D-AHLU

Boeing 737-5K5: D-AHLD, D-AHLE, D-AHLF, D-AHLI, D-AHLN

UK airports served: None regularly.

Above: **D-AHLS — Boeing 737-4K5 of Hapag-Lloyd.**

Heavylift Cargo Airlines (NP/HLA)   United Kingdom
Enterprise House, Stansted Airport, Essex   Tel: (01279) 680611

HeavyLift has specialised in carrying outsized loads since it began operations in March 1980 as TAC HeavyLift, a name which reflected the lingering ties with the defunct Transmeridian Air Cargo. In addition to the two remaining Belfasts, the airline also has the use of up to six Antonov An-124 Ruslan freighters in a joint venture with the Ukrainian company, VolgaDnepr. HeavyLift also flies cargo services on behalf of major carriers.

FLEET:

Antonov An-12: LZ-BAC, LZ-BAE, LZ-BAF

Antonov An-124: RA-82042, RA-82043, RA-82044, RA-82045, RA-82046, RA-82047

Ilyushin IL-76TD: RA-76401

Short SC5 Belfast: G-BEPS, G-HLFT

UK airports served: Glasgow, Manchester and Stansted; others as necessary for charters.

Above: **RA-82043 — Antonov An-124 of HeavyLift/VolgaDnepr.**

Hunting Cargo Airlines (AG/ABR)   United Kingdom
East Midlands Airport, Castle Donington, Leics   Tel: (01332) 811419

The airline is wholly owned by the Hunting Group but until September 1992 was known as Air Bridge Carriers. It is now one of the leading freight carriers in Europe with an extensive route network. Overnight parcel work is carried out for a variety of companies including DHL, Securicor and Parcelforce, but in addition cargo charters take the fleet to all parts of Europe, the Middle East and North Africa. Some of the aircraft, including the Boeing 727s, are registered to a subsidiary company trading as Hunting Cargo Airlines (Ireland).

Above: G-FIJV — L188CF Electra of Hunting Cargo Airlines.

FLEET:

Boeing 727-223: EI-HCB, EI-HCC, EI-HCD, EI-HCI

Boeing 727-225F: EI-HCA

Boeing 727-281F: EI-LCH, EI-TNT

L188PF Electra: G-FIJR

L188CF Electra: G-FIJV, G-FIZU, EI-CET, EI-CHW, EI-CHX, EI-CHZ, N360Q

UK airports served: Aberdeen, Belfast, Coventry, East Midlands, Edinburgh, Heathrow, Liverpool, Luton, Manchester and Southend.

Iberia (IB/IBE)   Spain
Calle Velazquez 130, Madrid E-28006   Tel: (1) 585 85 85

The present company was created from a collection of small airlines stretching back to 1921. Before World War 2 these carriers had operated on routes within Spain and to neighbouring countries, but such activities were severely affected after 1939 despite the nation's professed neutrality. Postwar services were re-established using DC-3s and DC-4s, while in September 1954 a transatlantic route was started with Super Constellations. Iberia re-equipped with Convair 440s in 1957 which then served until the next step took the airline into the jet age. At this point DC-8s arrived for the longer sectors, with the Convair giving way to the Caravelle, but the latter type did not remain for many years, since in June 1967 DC-9s began to join the carrier, marking the start of another round of modernisation. Iberia became an Airbus customer in 1981 when the first of six A300s entered service. By the end of the 1980s more fleet changes were planned with the result that MD87s and A320s began to replace the elderly DC-9s and Boeing 727s. In 1994 Iberia found itself in financial difficulty which led to a delay in the delivery of Boeing 757s and the cancellation of an order for the Airbus A321. Cargosur has been merged into the flag carrier and now operates as Iberia Cargo.

Above: **EC-FKH — Airbus A320-211 of Iberia.**

FLEET:

Airbus A300B4-120: EC-DLE, EC-DLF, EC-DLG, EC-DLH, EC-DNQ, EC-DNR

Airbus A300B4-203: EC-EON, EC-EOO

Airbus A320-211: EC-FAS, EC-FBQ, EC-FBR, EC-FBS, EC-FCB, EC-FDA, EC-FDB, EC-FEO, EC-FGH, EC-FGR, EC-FGU, EC-FGV, EC-FIA, EC-FIC, EC-FKD, EC-FKH, EC-FLP, EC-FLQ, EC-FML, EC-FMN, EC-FNR, EC-FQY

Airbus A340-313: EC-GGS, EC-, EC-

Boeing 727-256: EC-CBA, EC-CBF, EC-CBM, EC-CFA, EC-CFB, EC-CFC, EC-CFD, EC-CFE, EC-CFF, EC-CFG, EC-CFH, EC-CFI, EC-CFK, EC-CID, EC-CIE, EC-DCC, EC-DCD, EC-DCE, EC-DDV, EC-DDX, EC-DDY, EC-DDZ, EC-GCI, EC-GCJ, EC-GCK, EC-GCL, EC-GCM

Boeing 747-256B: EC-DIA, EC-DIB, EC-DLC, EC-DLD, EC-DNP, EC-EEK

Boeing 757-256: EC-FTR, EC-FXU, EC-FXV, EC-FYJ, EC-FYK, EC-FYL, EC-FYM, EC-FYN, EC-, EC-, EC-

Douglas DC-8-62F: EC-EMD, EC-EMX

Douglas DC-8-71F: EC-FVA

Douglas DC-9-32: EC-BIT

Douglas DC-9-34: EC-CTR, EC-CTT, EC-DGB

Douglas DC-10-30: EC-CBO, EC-CBP, EC-CEZ, EC-CLB, EC-DEA, EC-DHZ

McD Douglas MD87: EC-EUC, EC-EUD, EC-EUE, EC-EUL, EC-EVB, EC-EXF, EC-EXG, EC-EXM, EC-EXN, EC-EXR, EC-EXT, EC-EYB, EC-EYX, EC-EYY, EC-EYZ, EC-EZA, EC-EZS, EC-FEY, EC-FEZ, EC-FFA, EC-FFH, EC-FFI, EC-FHD, EC-FHK

UK airports served: Edinburgh, Gatwick, Heathrow, Leeds/Bradford and Manchester.

Icelandair (FI/ICE)	Iceland
IS-101 Reykjavik	Tel: (1) 69 10 00

Air transport in Iceland began in 1937 when Flugfelag Akureyrar was formed. Flying took place only in the summer months and these operations consisted of a domestic link between Reykjavik and Akureyri. The loss of its sole possession, a Waco YKS floatplane, caused some disruption in 1939, but in the following year another of the breed was acquired for Flugfelag Islands, the new name adopted by the airline. The domestic services were a lifeline for the isolated groups of inhabitants and produced sufficient traffic to warrant the creation of a second carrier known as Loftleidir.

Meanwhile Flugfelag had begun a service to Copenhagen and Glasgow using a leased 14-seat Liberator for the latter and a DC-3 for the Danish operation. By 1952 Loftleidir had decided to concentrate its energies on the international market, transferring its domestic activities to Icelandair, the title under which the pioneer company now traded. In 1973 the two carriers were merged although they continued to use their own identities until, in October 1979, the name Loftleidir was dropped.

There is little doubt that the Icelandic carriers did much to promote cheap transatlantic flights since the fare structure encouraged many cost-conscious travellers to use Iceland as a staging post. Nowadays, Icelandair operates domestic services to 10 destinations, while its international coverage includes most of the major European cities plus New York and Orlando in the US.

FLEET:

Boeing 737-408: TF-FIA, TF-FIB, TF-FIC, TF-FID
Boeing 757-28A: TF-FIK
Boeing 757-208: TF-FIH, TF-FII, TF-FIJ
Fokker 50: TF-FIR, TF-FIS, TF-FIT, TF-FIU

UK airports served: Glasgow and Heathrow.

InterLine (5W/GYP) — United Kingdom
Unit 5, Business Centre, Norwich Airport   Tel: (01603) 484594

The airline was founded in 1993 and began a twice-weekdaily service between its Norwich base and Manchester with a Jetstream 31. This sector was extended to Rotterdam in the spring of 1995 but dropped in November. A Norwich-Gatwick schedule was planned for a spring 1996 start, but the carrier was forced to suspend its activities before the launch.

Iran Air (IR/IRA) — Iran
PO Box 13185-775, Tehran   Tel: (21) 97 91 11

The merger of Persian Air Services and Iranian Airways was responsible for the creation of Iran Air in 1962. It became one of the world's fastest growing airlines with a network which spread far and wide to include such distant places as Tokyo and New York. Then came the rise to power of the Ayatollah Khomeini in 1979.

This political upheaval brought a speedy change of course for the airline, not to mention the even speedier departure of the Shah, under whose influence the company had prospered. The establishment of the Islamic Republic triggered off a considerable reduction in the weekly total of international departures, which quickly dropped from over 100 to under 30. At least the domestic schedules remained virtually intact as did the regional services with friendly neighbours. In 1980 a major disagreement with Iraq seriously affected Iran Air, which had to suspend many of its services while the holy men of the two countries waged a full-scale war. In the early 1990s Iran became a popular parking place for airliners seeking a safe haven when Iraq was the centre of attraction during the Gulf conflict. Iran Air currently operates a mix of Airbus, Boeing and Fokker products to 23 domestic destinations, while international flights link Tehran with a number of cities in Europe and the Middle and Far East.

FLEET:

Boeing 747SP-86: EP-IAA, EP-IAB, EP-IAC, EP-IAD

Boeing 747-186B: EP-IAM

Boeing 747-286B: EP-IAG, EP-IAH

Boeing 747-2J9F: EP-ICA, EP-ICC

Also operated are Airbus A300B4/A300-600, Boeing 707/727/737 and Fokker 100.

UK airport served: Heathrow.

Above: **EP-IAC — Boeing 747SP-86 of Iran Air.**

Isles of Scilly Skybus (FW/IOS)　　　United Kingdom
Land's End Aerodrome, St Just,
Penzance, Cornwall　　　Tel: (01736) 787017

Skybus began operations in August 1984 as a venture by the local shipping line. The company already offered regular sea crossings between the islands and Penzance, but decided to compete with the popular helicopter service. The carrier now flies year-round on the St Just-St Mary's sector, the frequency

Above: **G-SSKY — BN-2B-26 Islander of Isles of Scilly Skybus.**

varying with the seasons. Other routes to the Scillies are flown from Bristol, Exeter, Newquay and Plymouth, the latter pair during the summer season only. For some 10 years or so, the airline relied upon its Islander fleet to maintain the services, but in the spring of 1994 a Twin Otter was acquired to give extra capacity and comfort on the longer legs.

FLEET:

BN-2A Islander: G-SBUS
BN-2B Islander: G-BUBN, G-SSKY
DHC-6 Twin Otter 310: G-BIHD

UK airports served: Bristol, Exeter, Land's End, Newquay, Plymouth and St Mary's.

Istanbul Airlines (IL/IST)   Turkey
Firuzkoy Yolu 26, 34850 Avcilar-Istanbul   Tel: (212) 509 21 00

Below: **TC-AFR — Boeing 727-230 of Istanbul Airlines.**

After being formed in December 1985, the airline began operations during the following year by flying charters to European destinations. Some 56 points are now served which include most of the major cities.

FLEET:

Boeing 727-228: TC-AFB, TC-AFC	
Boeing 727-230: TC-AFN, TC-AFO, TC-AFP, TC-AFR, TC-AFT, TC-AFV	
Boeing 737-4S3: TV-APA, TC-AVA	
Boeing 737-4Y0: TC-ACA, TC-AGA, TC-AYA, TC-AZA	
Boeing 757-236: TC-AHA, TC-AJA	

UK airports served: Gatwick, Heathrow, Manchester and Stansted.

Japan Airlines (JL/JAL)	Japan
Tokyo Building, 7-3 Marunouchi, Chiyoda-ku, Tokyo 100	Tel: (3) 32 84 26 10

When Japan Airlines (JAL) was formed in August 1951, its activities were confined to the operation of domestic services. The airline was also forbidden to employ Japanese pilots, so the business was contracted to the US carrier Northwest Airlines. The privately owned JAL was reorganised in 1953 with the government securing a half share in the company. Links with America were started in February 1954, from which point the carrier expanded quickly and successfully at a time when the Japanese wartime partner in Europe had still to get airborne. The airline was privatised in November 1987 when the government disposed of its remaining 34.5% holding. In addition to its worldwide coverage, JAL also operates an intensive network of domestic schedules using the short-range variant of the Boeing 747. This type is employed on the high density shuttles, with the Series 400 version capable of accommodating over 560 passengers. The airline proposes to transfer some 20% of its international operations to its subsidiary, Japan Air Charter by 1998.

FLEET:

Boeing 747-212F: JA8193	
Boeing 747-221F: JA8160, JA8165	
Boeing 747-246B: JA8104, JA8105, JA8108, JA8113, JA8122, JA8125, JA8130, JA8131, JA8140, JA8141, JA8154, JA8161, JA8162, JA8169	
Boeing 747-246F: JA8123, JA8132, JA8171, N211JL	
Boeing 747-346: JA8163, JA8166, JA8173, JA8177, JA8178, JA8179, JA8185, N212JL, N213JL	
Boeing 747-446: JA8071, JA8072, JA8073, JA8074, JA8075, JA8076, JA8077, JA8078, JA8079, JA8080, JA8081, JA8082, JA8085, JA8086, JA8087, JA8088, JA8089, JA8901, JA8902, JA8906, JA8909, JA8910, JA8911, JA8912, JA8914	
Also operated are Boeing 747SRs, Boeing 767s, DC-10-40s and MD11s.	

UK airport served: Heathrow.

Above: YU-ANK — Boeing 737-3H9 of JAT.

The airline started operations in April 1947 with the assistance of the Soviet
Union. Unlike other beneficiaries, Yugoslavia tended to take a more
independent line, with the assets of the jointly-owned airline JUSTA being
transferred to JAT in 1949. Although remaining firmly state-owned, the airline
was allowed to develop routes throughout the western world. Unfortunately,
the civil war in the country grounded the carrier in the early 1990s, but control
eventually passed to Serbia. The government took 51% of the shares, offering
the remainder to the public. Nevertheless, sanctions imposed by the
United Nations still prevented JAT from resuming its activities for some time,
but a few domestic sectors and a limited number of international services were
revived in early 1995.

FLEET:

Boeing 727-2H9: YU-AKB, YU-AKE, YU-AKF, YU-AKG, YU-AKI, YU-AKJ

Boeing 737-3H9: YU-AND, YU-ANF, YU-ANH, YU-ANI, YU-ANJ, YU-ANK,
   YU-ANL, YU-ANV

Douglas DC-9-32: YU-AHN, YU-AHU, YU-AHV, YU-AJH, YU-AJI, YU-AJK, YU-AJL,
   YU-AJM

Douglas DC-10-30: YU-AMB

Also operated: Aérospatiale ATR72-201.

UK airport served: Heathrow.

Jersey European Airways (JY/JEA)   United Kingdom
Terminal Building, Exeter Airport, Devon   Tel: (01392) 364440

Jersey European was formed on 1 November 1979 to take over the services of the Channel Islands-based Intra Airways and the passenger work of Express Air Services headquartered at Bournemouth. Previously, Viscounts and DC-3s had been employed, but the new carrier considered that Islanders, Twin Otters and Bandeirantes were more appropriate for the type of services envisaged. Larger equipment was almost introduced in 1983, but the two Friendships due to join JEA were sold before delivery following a change of policy. After an uneasy period, the carrier emerged as a possession of the Walker Steel Group, already the owner of Blackpool-based Spacegrand. As a result, the activities of the two became integrated with all licences transferred to JEA in 1985. Earlier, the first of several Short SD3-30s had been delivered and these were followed in due course by the larger SD3-60. In 1988 two Friendship 500s were acquired for use on the busy Channel Islands routes, followed by six more of this variant in 1991. The airline introduced the BAe 146 to its trunk routes in 1993, using the type to serve Belfast and the Channel Islands from Gatwick plus a number of services from Birmingham. The network expanded still further in 1994 with the addition of the Stansted–Belfast sector, but on the debit side several of the thinner routes were quietly dropped.

FLEET:

BAe 146-100: G-JEAO
BAe 146-200: G-JEAJ, G-JEAK, G-JEAR, G-JEAS
BAe 146-300: G-JEAL, G-JEAM
F27 Friendship Mk 500: G-JEAD, G-JEAE, G-JEAF, G-JEAG, G-JEAH, G-JEAI, G-JEAP
Short SD3-60 Variant 100: G-OBHD, G-OBLK

UK airports served: Belfast, Birmingham, Blackpool, Bristol, Exeter, Gatwick, Guernsey, Isle of Man, Jersey, Leeds/Bradford, Manchester and Stansted.

Below: **G-JEAL — BAe 146-300 of Jersey European Airways.**

Kenya Airways (KQ/KQA)   Kenya
PO Box 19002, Nairobi   Tel: (2) 82 21 71

The airline was created by the Kenyan government in January 1977 due to the sudden demise of East African Airways. It introduced a daily service to London on 4 February 1977, initially using Boeing 707s leased from British Midland. Later the carrier obtained its own aircraft and now operates scheduled regional and international services from Nairobi and Mombasa to a variety of European and African destinations.

FLEET:

Airbus A310-304: 5Y-BEL, 5Y-BEN, 5Y-BFT

Also operated are Boeing 737s and Fokker 50s.

UK airport served: Heathrow.

Kibris Turkish Airlines (YK/KYV)   North Cyprus
Bedredden Demirel Avenue,
Yenisehir, Nicosia, North Cyprus   Tel: 228 39 01

Above: TC-JYK — Airbus A310-203 of Kibris Turkish Airlines

Since the Turkish Republic of Northern Cyprus is only recognised by Turkey, not surprisingly the country's flag carrier has a large shareholding and supplies aircraft when the need arises. Known as Cyprus Turkish Airlines when operations started in February 1975, the present name was later adopted.

FLEET:

Airbus A310-203: TC-JYK

Airbus A310-304: TC-TMT

Boeing 727-2F2: TC-JBG, TC-JBJ

Boeing 727-228: TC-JEC

UK airport served: Stansted.

KLM – Royal Dutch Airlines (KL/KLM)　Netherlands
PO Box 7700. NL-1117 ZL Schiphol-Oost　　Tel: (20) 649 91 23

Since it was formed as early as 7 October 1919, KLM has the distinction of being the oldest operating airline in the world. Services began on 17 May 1920 with a link between Amsterdam and London, a trip which quickly grew into a twice-daily operation. The company's association with the Douglas DC-2 and -3 took it to the forefront of the European carriers, a position it later maintained by re-equipping with Convairs, Viscounts and Electras in the 1950s and 1960s. These in turn were replaced by the DC-9 which served in large numbers until the late 1980s when the Boeing 737-300 took over the European routes. Regional services are operated by the flag carrier's subsidiary KLM CityHopper (previously NLM CityHopper) using Fokker F50s, F70s and SAAB SF340s.

FLEET:

Boeing 737-306: PH-BDA, PH-BDB, PH-BDC, PH-BDD, PH-BDE, PH-BDG, PH-BDH, PH-BDI, PH-BDK, PH-BDL, PH-BDN, PH-BDO, PH-BDP, PH-BTD, PH-BTE

Boeing 737-406: PH-BDR, PH-BDS, PH-BDT, PH-BDU, PH-BDW, PH-BDY, PH-BDZ, PH-BTA, PH-BTB, PH-BTC, PH-BTF, PH-BTG

Boeing 737-42C: G-UKLC, G-UKLD, G-UKLF, G-UKLG

Boeing 747-306: PH-BUH, PH-BUI, PH-BUK, PH-BUL, PH-BUM, PH-BUN, PH-BUO, PH-BUP, PH-BUR, PH-BUT, PH-BUU, PH-BUV, PH-BUW

Above: **PH-BTB — Boeing 737-406 of KLM.**

Boeing 747-406: PH-BFA, PH-BFB, PH-BFC, PH-BFD, PH-BFE, PH-BFF, PH-BFG, PH-BFH, PH-BFI, PH-BFK, PH-BFL, PH-BFM, PH-BFN, PH-BFO, PH-BFP, PH-BFR, PH-BFS, PH-BFT

Boeing 767-306ER: PH-BZA, PH-BZB, PH-BZC, PH-BZD, PH-BZE, PH-BZF, PH-BZG, PH-BZH, PH-BZI, PH-BZK, PH-BZL

McD Douglas MD11: PH-KCA, PH-KCB, PH-KCC, PH-KCD, PH-KCE, PH-KCF, PH-KCG, PH-KCH, PH-KCI, PH-KCK

CITYHOPPER

Fokker 50: PH-KVA, PH-KVB, PH-KVC, PH-KVD, PH-KVE, PH-KVF, PH-KVG, PH-KVH, PH-KVI, PH-KVK

Fokker 70: PH-KZA, PH-KZB, PH-KZC, PH-KZD

SAAB SF340B: PH-KSA, PH-KSB, PH-KSC, PH-KSD, PH-KSE, PH-KSF, PH-KSG, PH-KSI, PH-KSK, PH-KSL, PH-KSM

UK airports served: Belfast, Birmingham, Bristol, Cardiff, Guernsey, Heathrow, Jersey and Southampton.

Korean Air (KE/KAL) — Korea

CPO Box 864, 41-3 Seosomun-dong, Chung-gu, Seoul

Tel: (2) 751 71 14

The airline was founded in 1962 to succeed Korean National Airlines which had started operations in 1948. Although Korean Air provides two domestic routes, its main activity involves international schedules which include seven European destinations.

FLEET:

Boeing 747-4B5: HL7472, HL7473, HL7477, HL7478, HL7479, HL7480, HL7481, HL7482, HL7483, HL7484, HL7485, HL7486, HL7487, HL7488, HL7489, HL7490, HL7491, HL7492, HL7493, HL7494, HL7495, HL7496, HL7498

Boeing 747-4B5F: HL7497

Also operated are Airbus A300, A330, Boeing 727, Boeing 747-200, Fokker 100 and MD82.

UK airport served: Heathrow.

Kuwait Airways (KU/KAC) — Kuwait

PO Box 394, Kuwait

Tel: 434 46 37

Kuwait National Airways was formed in March 1953 with the assistance of BOAC. A service was started in 1954 using a pair of DC-3s on a route to Basra, the British company providing both crews and maintenance. National was dropped from the title during the following year, whereupon the government became joint owners of the airline until gaining full control in 1962. From this point the route network was greatly expanded, with European destinations added in 1964. Kuwait Airways became the first customer for the convertible

Above: **9K-ANA — Airbus A340-313 of Kuwait Airways.**

version of the A300-600 to operate alongside its five A310s. During the Gulf problems in the early 1990s, a number of the carrier's aircraft were seized by Iraq and subsequently replaced when peace was restored.

FLEET:

Airbus A300-605R: 9K-AMA, 9K-AMB, 9K-AMC, 9K-AMD, 9K-AME
Airbus A310-308: 9K-ALA, 9K-ALB, 9K-ALC, 9K-ALD
Airbus A340-313: 9K-ANA, 9K-ANB, 9K-ANC, 9K-AND
Boeing 747-269B: 9K-ADA, 9K-ADB, 9K-ADC, 9K-ADD
Boeing 747-469: 9K-ADE, 9K-ADF, 9K-ADG

UK airport served: Heathrow.

L'Aéropostale (ARP) — France
BP 10454, F-95708 Roissy-Charles de Gaulle — Tel: (1) 40 32 44 12

Below: **F-GIXG — Boeing 737-382QC of L'Aéropostale.** *A. S. Wright*

This company was known as Intercargo Service when it began operations in 1987, but subsequently the name was changed to L'Aéropostale. Using a number of Boeing 737s, the airline is involved in the nightly transport of mail and also general cargo charters.

FLEET:

Boeing 727-225F: F-GKDY, F-GKDZ	
Boeing 737-230C: F-GFVI	
Boeing 737-2K2C: F-GGVP, F-GGVQ, F-GIXA	
Boeing 737-348QC: F-GIXI, F-GIXL	
Boeing 737-382QC: F-GIXG	
Boeing 737-33AQC: F-GIXB, F-GIXD	
Boeing 737-38BQC: F-GIXC	
Boeing 737-3B3QC: F-GFUE, F-GFUF, F-GIXE, F-GIXF	
Boeing 737-3M8: F-GIXP	
Boeing 737-3Q8F: F-GIXM, F-GIXO	
Boeing 737-3S3F: G-GIXH	
Boeing 737-3Y0F: F-GIXJ, F-GIXK	

UK airports served: Gatwick and Heathrow.

Laker Airways (6F)   USA
1100 Lee Wagner Boulevard, Suite 209A,
Fort Lauderdale, FL 33315   Tel: (305) 359 7609

The airline was formed by Sir Freddie Laker in May 1992 to provide charter flights between the US and Grand Bahamas with Boeing 727s. Subsequently these became scheduled services, at the same time expanding away from the Florida region. Preparations began in 1995 for the launch of transatlantic charters, approval for which was received to permit the first flights to be made in the spring of 1996.

FLEET:

Douglas DC-10-30: N831LA, N832LA, N833LA	

UK airports served: Gatwick and Manchester.

Lauda Air (NG/LDA)   Austria
PO Box 56, Lauda Air Building,
A-1300 Wien-Schwechat   Tel: (1) 711 10 20 81

Lauda Air was formed in 1979 by former racing driver Niki Lauda to operate charter and air-taxi services with a pair of Friendships. The airline expanded its activities in the mid-1980s by leasing One-Elevens from Tarom to offer IT flights to the Mediterranean. Lauda received approval to operate scheduled services in 1987, followed by licences covering international flights in 1990. A subsidiary company (Lauda Air SpA) is based at Milan and employs a Boeing 767 for long-haul charters.

FLEET:

Boeing 737-3Z9: OE-ILF, OE-ILG

Boeing 737-4Z9: OE-LNH, OE-LNI

Boeing 767-3Z9ER: OE-LAU, OE-LAW, OE-LAX

Boeing 767-31AER: OE-LAT

Boeing 767-33AER: OE-LAS

Canadair Regional Jet 100ER: OE-LRA, OE-LRB, OE-LRC, OE-LRD, OE-LRE, OE-LRF, OE-LRG, OE-LRHUK airports served: Gatwick, Glasgow and Manchester.

UK airport served: Heathrow.

Above: **OE-LNH — Boeing 737-4Z9 of Lauda Air.** *A. S. Wright*

Leisure International Airways (UK/ULE) United Kingdom
Apollo House, Lowfield Heath, Surrey   Tel: (01279) 680737

The company was formed in 1993 as an affiliate of Air UK Leisure to operate long-haul charters for Unijet, the owner of the airline. Operations started with two Boeing 767s in 1993, the aircraft thereafter being used on regular transatlantic charters to the Caribbean area from Gatwick and Manchester. In 1996 the company absorbed Air UK Leisure, at the same time replacing the latter's Boeing 737 fleet with Airbus A320, as an interim measure pending delivery of the first A321 in Spring 1997.

FLEET:

Airbus A320-212: G-UKLJ, G-UKLK, G-UKLL

Airbus A321-200: G-, G-, G-, G-

Boeing 767-39HER: G-UKLH, G-UKLI

UK airports served: Belfast, Birmingham, Gatwick, Glasgow, Manchester, Prestwick and Stansted.

Lithuanian Airlines (TE/LIL)
8 Radunes, Vilnius Airport, Vilnius

Lithuania
Tel: (2) 63 01 16

When the Baltic state became independent of the Soviet Union, Lithuanian Airlines was formed to take over the services previously operated by Aeroflot. A single Boeing 737-200 was leased to begin the change to Western equipment, this machine operating most of the schedules.

FLEET:

Boeing 737-2Q8: LY-GPA

Boeing 737-2T2: LY-BSG

Boeing 737-2T4: LY-BSD

Tupolev Tu-134A-3: LY-ABB, LY-ABE, LY-ABF, LY-ABG, LY-ABI

Yakovlev Yak-42: LY-AAM, LY-AAO, LY-AAQ, LY-AAR, LY-AAS, LY-AAT, LY-AAU, LY-AAV, LY-AAW, LY-AAX

UK airport served: Heathrow.

Above: **LY-GPA — Boeing 737-2Q8 of Lithuanian Airlines.**

Loganair (LC/LOG)
St Andrews Drive, Glasgow Abbotsinch Airport, Paisley

United Kingdom
Tel: (0141) 889 1311

Loganair was formed in 1962 as the aviation division of Duncan Logan Ltd, a civil engineering group, principally to transport directors and staff to construction sites and meetings. Subsequently, the demand for its services prompted expansion and its entry into the scheduled business. Most of the

Above: **G-BLGB — Short SD3-60 of Loganair/British Airways**

early activities provided vital links for the islands off the Scottish coast, with the airline later taking the responsibility for the Air Ambulance Service previously in the hands of BEA. Through the years Loganair expanded its operations across the border, at the same time increasing its fleet to include larger capacity types such as the ATP and BAe 146. It became a subsidiary of British Midland in September 1983 and a member of the Airlines of Britain Group in December 1987. The latter carried out a major reorganisation in early 1994 which resulted in Loganair transferring routes and aircraft to Manx. Most of the remaining services were internal Scottish routes and flown by Islanders and Short SD3-60s, some of which were ex-Manx machines. In July 1994 Loganair signed a franchise agreement with British Airways with the result that most of the aircraft were repainted in BA livery and flight codes were those of the national carrier. A further change in October 1996 resulted in Loganair flying as British Regional Airlines.

FLEET:

BN-2B Islander: G-BJOP, G-BLNJ, G-BLNW, G-BPCA

DHC-6 Twin Otter 310: G-BVVK

Short SD3-60 Variant 100: G-BKMX, G-BLGB, G-BMAR, G-BVMY, G-ISLE, G-LEGS, G-WACK

UK airports served: Aberdeen, Barra, Belfast, Campbeltown, Edinburgh, Glasgow, Inverness, Islay, Londonderry, Kirkwall, Sumburgh and Wick plus others on the Scottish islands.

LOT-Polish Airlines (LO/LOT)　　　　　Poland
17 Stycznia Street 39, Warsaw PL-00908　　　Tel: (2) 630 06 75

On 1 January 1929 civil air transport activities were taken over by the Polish government which duly formed Polskie Linie Lotnicze (LOT). Various routes were introduced and by 1939 the airline was serving Croydon with its modern DC-2s. Plans were well advanced for a service to South America when World War 2 delayed LOT's development for six years.

Surprisingly, Poland was the first eastern European country to re-establish its airline industry after the war. Before the end of 1945 a London service had been started, Russian-built Li-2s forming the new fleet. It also became the first of the communist-influenced nations to buy Western-built aircraft when it acquired Convair 240s and Viscounts. However, Russian pressure later ensured that the airline used Soviet products again for some years. With the end of the Soviet domination, LOT began to re-equip its fleet with Boeing 737s and 767s in the early 1990s and now uses these aircraft for its scheduled services.

FLEET:

Boeing 737-3Q8: SP-LMB

Boeing 737-45D: SP-LLA, SP-LLB, SP-LLC, SP-LLD, SP-LLE

Boeing 737-55D: SP-LKA, SP-LKB, SP-LKC, SP-LKD, SP-LKE, SP-LKF

Boeing 767-25DER: SP-LOA, SP-LOB

Boeing 767-35DER: SP-LPA, SP-LPB

Also operated are Aérospatiale ATR72-202.

UK airport served: Heathrow.

LTE International Airways (XO/LTE)   Spain
Calle de Ter 27, 07009 Palma de Mallorca   Tel: (71) 41 94 00

The airline was formed in April 1987 to operate charters from mainland Spain and its islands to various European cities. It is wholly owned by the German carrier LTU and uses a similar livery for its aircraft.

FLEET:

Boeing 757-2G5: EC-EFX, EC-EGH, EC-ENQ

UK airports served: None regularly.

LTU-Lufttransport-Unternehmen (LT/LTU)   Germany
Halle 8, Flughafen Düsseldorf, D-40474 Düsseldorf   Tel: (211) 92 18 08

The airline was formed as a charter operator equipped with Vikings, but in the early 1960s the carrier did in fact undertake some third-level scheduled services for Lufthansa. LTU's fleet moved through Friendships and Fellowships and a lengthy period with Caravelles before standardising on the TriStar for both charters and schedules. This type has since spent much of its time ferrying holidaymakers to the Mediterranean resorts, but after years of reliable service the airline began re-equipping with the MD11 and the Airbus A330 in 1994.

FLEET:

Airbus A330-321: D-AERF, D-AERG, D-AERH, D-AERJ, D-AERK, D-AERQ, D-AE

McD Douglas MD11: D-AERB, D-AERW, D-AERX, D-AERZ

UK airports served: None regularly.

LTU Sud International Airways — Germany
PO Box 231844, D-85327 München Tel: (89) 97 810

This German charter carrier was formed in 1983 as Lufttransport Sud, but adopted the present title in January 1988. It is a member of the LTU Group and undertakes both short- and long-haul charters. The fleet uses the same red livery as its partners LTE and LTU.

FLEET:

Boeing 757-2G5: D-AMUM, D-AMUQ, D-AMUV, D-AMUW, D-AMUX, D-AMUY, D-AMUZ

Boeing 757-225: D-AMUK, D-AMUU

Boeing 757-236: D-AMUL

Boeing 767-3G5ER: D-AMUN, D-AMUR, D-AMUS

Boeing 767-33AER: D-AMUP

UK airports served: None regularly.

Above: **D-AMUW — Boeing 757-2G5 of LTU Sud.**

Lufthansa (LH/DLH) — Germany
Von Gablenz Strasse 2-6, D-5000 Köln Tel: (221) 82 60

Germany's flag carrier can trace its history back to January 1926 when Deutsche Luft Hansa was formed by merging Aero Lloyd and Junkers Luftverkehr. The new company began its commercial life on 6 April and rapidly became an airline of considerable strength in the world, contributing much to the pioneering of new routes.

Above: D-ABID — Boeing 737-530 of Lufthansa.

With the outbreak of war in 1939, civil transport flights were curtailed to some extent, but by no means suspended, since most of Europe soon came under German control anyway. After a short pause, DLH was able to resume flights to the Balkan countries, Italy, Portugal, Scandinavia and Spain. In fact, as early as mid-August 1940 the airline opened its longest and probably one of the most important routes to Madrid via Lyon, Marseille and Barcelona. An extension to Lisbon was introduced in October and it was here that DLH machines mingled with those of BOAC, both carriers being generously supplied with a constant stream of secret agents masquerading as passengers. The airline's final schedule was operated by a Focke-Wulf Condor on 21 April 1945 flying the Berlin–Munich–Madrid route, although the aircraft failed to reach its destination for reasons never discovered.

It was January 1953 before a start was made to launch a new German airline after the war. Luftag was the name for a short time during the preparatory work, but on 6 August 1954 the old company title of Deutsche Luft Hansa was resurrected, although the initials DLH were no longer used. Domestic services started on 1 April 1955, followed quickly by international links. By the end of the year not only were most of the European capitals included in the network, but Super Constellations were already visiting New York.

Lufthansa was truly emulating its famous forebear with its speed of growth and the choice of equipment. The airline became an early customer for the Boeing 727 and the first for the smaller 737, variants of which have since been the mainstay of the fleet. In later years, the company contributed much to the Airbus designs and, with Swissair, became the launch customer for the A310. Subsequently it has ordered other products from the European consortium including the A320, A321 and A340. Lufthansa CityLine, Condor Flugdienst and Lufthansa Cargo are subsidiaries of the company. The B737-400s are to be sold in 1997.

FLEET:

Airbus A300-605: D-AIAH, D-AIAI, D-AIAK, D-AIAL, D-AIAM, D-AIAN, D-AIAP, D-AIAR, D-AIAS, D-AIAT, D-AIAU, D-AIAW

Airbus A310-304: D-AIDA, D-AIDC, D-AIDD, D-AIDE, D-AIDF, D-AIDH, D-AIDI, D-AIDK, D-AIDL, D-AIDM, D-AIDN

Airbus A319-114: D-AILA, D-AILB, D-AILC, D-AILD, D-AILE, D-AILF, D-AILH, D-AILI, D-AILK, D-AILL, D-AILM

Airbus A320-211: D-AIPA, D-AIPB, D-AIPC, D-AIPD, D-AIPE, D-AIPF, D-AIPH, D-AIPK, D-AIPL, D-AIPM, D-AIPP, D-AIPR, D-AIPS, D-AIPT, D-AIPU, D-AIPW, D-AIPX, D-AIPY, D-AIPZ, D-AIQA, D-AIQB, D-AIQC, D-AIQD, D-AIQE, D-AIQF, D-AIQH, D-AIQK, D-AIQL, D-AIQM, D-AIQN, D-AIQP, D-AIQR, D-AIQS

Airbus A321-131: D-AIRA, D-AIRB, D-AIRC, D-AIRD, D-AIRE, D-AIRF, D-AIRH, D-AIRK, D-AIRL, D-AIRM, D-AIRN, D-AIRO, D-AIRP, D-AIRR, D-AIRS, D-AIRT, D-AIRU, D-AIRV, D-AIRW, D-AIRX, D-AIRY

Airbus A340-211: D-AIBA, D-AIBC, D-AIBD, D-AIBE, D-AIBF, D-AIBH

Airbus A340-311: D-AIGA, D-AIGB, D-AIGC, D-AIGD, D-AIGF, D-AIGH, D-AIGI, D-AIGK, D-AIGL, D-AIGM

Boeing 737-230: D-ABFA, D-ABFB, D-ABFP, D-ABFR, D-ABFU, D-ABFW, D-ABFX, D-ABHC, D-ABHF, D-ABHH, D-ABHM, D-ABHN, D-ABMA, D-ABMB, D-ABMC, D-ABMD, D-ABME, D-ABMF

Boeing 737-330: D-ABEA, D-ABEB, D-ABEC, D-ABED, D-ABEE, D-ABEF, D-ABEH, D-ABEI, D-ABEK, D-ABEL, D-ABEM, D-ABEN, D-ABEO, D-ABEP, D-ABER, D-ABES, D-ABET, D-ABEU, D-ABEW, D-ABWC, D-ABWD, D-ABWE, D-ABWF, D-ABWH, D-ABXA, D-ABXB, D-ABXC, D-ABXD, D-ABXE, D-ABXF, D-ABXH, D-ABXI, D-ABXK, D-ABXL, D-ABXM, D-ABXN, D-ABXO, D-ABXP, D-ABXR, D-ABXS, D-ABXT, D-ABXU, D-ABXW, D-ABXX, D-ABXY, D-ABXZ

Boeing 737-3S3: D-ABWS

Boeing 737-430: D-ABKA, D-ABKB, D-ABKC, D-ABKD, D-ABKF, D-ABKK

Boeing 737-530: D-ABIA, D-ABIB, D-ABIC, D-ABID, D-ABIE, D-ABIF, D-ABIH, D-ABII, D-ABIK, D-ABIL, D-ABIM, D-ABIN, D-ABIO. D-ABIP, D-ABIR, D-ABIS, D-ABIT, D-ABIU, D-ABIW, D-ABIX, D-ABIY, D-ABIZ, D-ABJA, D-ABJB, D-ABJC, D-ABJD, D-ABJE, D-ABJF, D-ABJH, D-ABJI

Boeing 747-230B: D-ABYM, D-ABYP, D-ABYQ, D-ABYR, D-ABYX, D-ABZD, D-ABZH

Boeing 747-230F: D-ABYO, D-ABYT, D-ABYU, D-ABYW, D-ABYY, D-ABYZ, D-ABZA, D-ABZB, D-ABZC, D-ABZF, D-ABZI

Boeing 747-430: D-ABTA, D-ABTB, D-ABTC, D-ABTD, D-ABTE, D-ABTF, D-ABTH, D-ABVA, D-ABVB, D-ABVC, D-ABVD, D-ABVE, D-ABVF, D-ABVH, D-ABVK, D-ABVL, D-ABVN, D-ABVO

UK airports served: Birmingham, Gatwick, Heathrow, Jersey and Manchester.

Lufthansa CityLine (CL/CLH) — Germany
Postfach 1111, Am Holzweg 26, D-65830 Kriftel   Tel: (6192) 40 70

The carrier was formed as Ostfriesische Lufttaxi (OLT) in 1958 for charter work. It was reorganised in 1974 when it became known as DLT using Friendships for passenger and freight work. The company was also contracted to fly domestic

Above: **D-ACJC — Canadair Regional Jet 100ER of Lufthansa CityLine.**

services for Lufthansa, eventually becoming a wholly-owned subsidiary of the flag carrier with the new title of Lufthansa CityLine in 1992. The airline is now responsible for its parent's European flights requiring up to 100 seats, for which purpose it ordered the Avro RJ to operate alongside its Canadair Regional Jets.

FLEET:

Avro RJ85: D-AVRA, D-AVRB, D-AVRC, D-AVRD, D-AVRE, D-AVRF, D-AVRG, D-AVRH, D-AVRI, D-AVRJ, D-AVRK, D-AVRL, D-AVRM, D-AVRN, D-AVRO, D-AVRP, D-AVRQ

Canadair Regional Jet 100ER: D-ACJA, D-ACJB, D-ACJC, D-ACJD, D-ACJA, D-ACJB, D-ACJC, D-ACJD, D-ACLA, D-ACLB, D-ACLC, D-ACLD, D-ACLE, D-ACLF, D-ACLG, D-ACLH, D-ACLI, D-ACLJ, D-ACLK, D-ACLL, D-ACLM, D-ACLN, D-ACLO, D-ACLP, D-ACLQ, D-ACLR, D-ACLS, D-ACLT, D-ACLU, D-ACLV, D-ACLW, D-ACLX, D-ACLY, D-ACLZ

UK airports served: Birmingham, Glasgow, Guernsey, Jersey and Manchester.

Luxair (LG/LGL)   Luxembourg

BP 2203, Aéroport de Luxembourg,
L-2987 Luxembourg   Tel: 47 98 23 11

Luxair's operational career started on 2 April 1962, having taken over as the national carrier from Luxembourg Airlines. Scheduled services were introduced using a leased Friendship, the type becoming the mainstay of the fleet for over 25 years. Longer-range activities are handled by Boeing 737s, many of the flights being ITs to the Mediterranean and Canary Islands. Scheduled commuter services are operated on behalf of its parent company by Luxair Commuter using three Brasilias for the duties.

FLEET:

Boeing 737-4C9: LX-LGF, LX-LGG

Boeing 737-5C9: LX-LGO, LX-LGP

EMB-120ER Brasilia: LX-LGK, LX-LGL, LX-LGM

Above: **LX-LGC — Fokker 50 of Luxair.**

Fokker 50: LX-LGB, LX-LGC, LX-LGD, LX-LGE

UK airports served: Heathrow, Manchester and Stansted.

Maersk Air (DM/DMA) — Denmark
Copenhagen Airport South, DK-2791 Dragoer — Tel: (32) 45 44 44

The large Maersk Line shipping group formed its own airline in 1969, using Friendships for general IT and charter work. By the mid-1970s these had given way to a fleet of Boeing 720s enabling the carrier to operate longer-range services for the Scandinavian travel industry. Gradually this type was supplemented and finally replaced in 1981 by Boeing 737s. In addition to its IT network, Maersk is also a major scheduled service carrier with both domestic and international routes. The company specialises in leasing members of its large fleet to other airlines for long- and short-term periods.

FLEET:

Boeing 737-3L9: OY-MAR, OY-MAS, OY-MAT, OY-MAU

Boeing 737-5L9: OY-MAC, OY-MAD, OY-MAE, OY-APA, OY-APB, OY-APC, OY-APD, OY-, OY-

Below: **OY-MAT — Boeing 737-3L9 of Maersk Air.**

Fokker 50: OY-MBM, OY-MMG, OY-MMH, OY-MMI, OY-MMJ, OY-MMS, OY-MMT, OY-MMU, OY-MMV

UK airports served: Birmingham, Gatwick, Manchester and Stansted.

Maersk Air Ltd (VB/BEA)   United Kingdom
Maersk Air House, 2245-49 Coventry Road,
Birmingham   Tel: (0121) 743 9090

The company was created from the split of Brymon European on 1 August 1993, barely a year after the merger of Brymon Airways and Birmingham European. The BEA element of the carrier was bought by Maersk Air, while Brymon became a wholly-owned subsidiary of British Airways. It was the first time that a company had taken advantage of the European Union's rule that allows 100% foreign ownership of a UK airline. Maersk has continued the same services as its predecessor, but operates under a BA franchise agreement with the aircraft in the flag carrier's livery.

FLEET:

BAC One-Eleven 501EX: G-AWYR, G-AWYS, G-AWYV

BAe Jetstream 41: G-MSKJ

Boeing 737-5L9: G-MSKA, G-MSKB, G-MSKC

UK airports served: Belfast, Birmingham and Newcastle.

Malaysia Airlines (MH/MAS)   Malaysia
Jalan Sultan Ismail, Bangunan MAS,
50250 Kuala Lumpur   Tel: (3) 746 45 55

Above: **9M-MPE — Boeing 747-4H6 of Malaysia Airlines.**

The national carrier of Malaysia has had a number of name changes and associations with other airlines since it was started in 1947. BOAC and Qantas were the majority shareholders in the early days until the governments of Malaysia and Singapore gained joint control in 1966. A year later it was renamed Malaysia-Singapore Airlines, but this alliance lasted only until the early 1970s. Malaysian Airline System was then formed, this identity lasting until 1987 when the present title was adopted.

FLEET:

Boeing 747-4H6: 9M-MHL, 9M-MHM, 9M-MHN, 9M-MHO, 9M-MPA, 9M-MPB, 9M-MPC, 9M-MPD, 9M-MPE, 9M-MPF, 9M-MPG, 9M-MPH, 9M-MPI	
Also operated are Airbus A300/A330, Boeing 737/747-200/300, DC-10-30 and Fokker 50.	

UK airport served: Heathrow.

Malev (MA/MAH)   Hungary
Roosevelt Ter 2, H-1051 Budapest   Tel: (1) 266 90 33

The Soviet Union played a large part in reshaping the country's air transport system after the war. Maszovlet was formed as a result, starting its first services from Budapest in October 1946. Progress was slow for the next few years, until in 1954 the Hungarian government was able to buy Russia's half share in the airline which was renamed Magyar Legikozlekedesi Vallalat (Malev). The company ceased its domestic activities in 1969 in an attempt to expand its international coverage. Schedules are now flown to a large number of cities in Europe and the Middle East with a fleet which has steadily lost its Russian influence to become largely equipped with Western-built equipment.

FLEET:

Boeing 737-2K9: HA-LEK
Boeing 737-2M8: HA-LEB
Boeing 737-2Q8: HA-LEA
Boeing 737-2T4: HA-LEI, HA-LEM
Boeing 737-2T5: HA-LEC
Boeing 737-3Q8: HA-LEJ
Boeing 737-3Y0: HA-LED, HA-LEF, HA-LEG
Boeing 737-4Y0: HA-LEN, HA-LEO
Boeing 767-27GER: HA-LHA, HA-LHB
Fokker 70: HA-LMA, HA-LMB, HA-LMC, HA-LMD
Also operated are Tupolev Tu-134 and Tu-154s.

UK airport served: Heathrow.

Manx Airlines (JE/MNX)   United Kingdom
Ronaldsway Airport, Ballasalla, Isle of Man   Tel : (01624) 826000

After a gap of some 24 years, Manx was revived in 1982 following a joint venture by British Midland and Air UK, each supplying an aircraft to permit services to begin later that year. Both carriers transferred their Isle of Man routes to Manx which found traffic figures climbing steadily as local travellers supported the airline. A direct London service was flown for some years with a

Above: **G-MANA — BAe ATP of Manx Airlines.**

Viscount, but this was replaced by a BAe 146 in 1987.

Later, as a member of the Airlines of Britain Group, the company's operations were split into two separate divisions, namely Manx Airlines and Manx Airlines (Europe). Further changes came in March 1994 when the non-Scottish routes flown by Loganair were transferred, thereby producing a considerably expanded network. From January 1995, Manx Airlines (Europe) began operating as a British Airways Express carrier after signing a franchise agreement. Routes radiating from the Isle of Man were not included in the change and remain the responsibility of Manx Airlines. In October 1996 Manx Europe became a part of British Regional Airlines and took over BA's remaining Highlands services.

FLEET:

BAe 146-200: G-MANS, G-MIMA	
BAe ATP: G-MANA, G-MANB, G-MANC, G-MANE, G-MANF, G-MANG, G-MANH, G-MANJ, G-MANL, G-MANM, G-MANO, G-MANP, G-MAUD	
BAe Jetstream 31: G-GLAM, G-LOGV	
BAe Jetstream 41: G-MAJA, G-MAJB, G-MAJC, G-MAJD, G-MAJE, G-MAJF, G-MAJG, G-MAJH, G-MAJI, G-MAJJ, G-MAJM	

UK airports served: Aberdeen, Belfast, Birmingham, Cardiff, Edinburgh, Glasgow, Guernsey, Heathrow, Isle of Man, Jersey, Liverpool, Leeds/Bradford, Luton, Manchester, Newcastle, Southampton and Stansted.

Martinair (MP/MPH)　　　　Netherlands

Martinair Building, PO Box 7507,
NL-1118 Schiphol Airport　　　　Tel: (20) 601 12 22

The airline was formed as Martin's Air Charter in May 1958 using leased aircraft as required. As business grew, so it became necessary for the company to

Above: **PH-MCE — Boeing 747-21AC of Martinair.**

acquire its own machines for both passenger and freight charters. During the 1960s several shipping companies took an interest, an example also followed by KLM. One of the benefits of the latter brought the transfer of a pair of DC-7s and a Convair 340 from the national carrier to greatly increase MAC's range of activities.

Subsequently, the airline has employed a number of wide-bodied machines for its contracted work, including Boeing 747s, Airbus A310s, Boeing 767s and DC-10s, the latter now replaced by MD11s. Its freight services take the fleet worldwide, while IT charters are flown for the Dutch travel industry to the Mediterranean and Canary Islands throughout the year.

FLEET:

Boeing 747-21AC: PH-MCE, PH-MCF	
Boeing 747-228F: PH-MCN	
Boeing 767-31AER: PH-MCG, PH-MCH, PH-MCI, PH-MCL, PH-MCM, PH-MCV	
McD Douglas MD11CF: PH-MCP, PH-MCR, PH-MCS, PH-MCT, PH-MCU	

UK airports served: Birmingham and Stansted.

Meridiana (IG/ISS) — Italy
193 Corso Umberto, I-07026 Olbia, Sardinia — Tel: (789) 52 600

When formed in 1963 the airline was known as Alisarda, the name remaining in use until September 1991 when Meridiana was introduced. At first the carrier concentrated on charter work for the holiday industry, but in 1966 it began scheduled services to link the island with the mainland. Nowadays Meridiana provides regular services to a number of Italian cities, in addition to year-round and seasonal operations to other European airports.

FLEET:

BAe 146-200: I-FLRE, I-FLRI, I-FLRO, I-FLRU	
Douglas DC-9-51: I-SMEA, I-SMEE, I-SMEI, I-SMEJ, I-SMEO, I-SMEU	

McD Douglas MD82: I-SMEI, I-SMEM, I-SMEP, I-SMER, I-SMES, I-SMET, I-SMEV, PH-SEZ

UK airport served: Gatwick.

Middle East Airlines (ME/MEA) — Lebanon
PO Box 206 Beirut   Tel: (1) 31 63 16

Operations started modestly in 1945 with a few regional services flown by Rapides. These were replaced by the larger DC-2 after two years or so, but it was not long before the familiar pattern of political unrest began to emerge. Despite the decidedly unhealthy situation in the area surrounding its base, the airline somehow managed to continue its operations. It was not without loss or damage, however. One of the worst incidents occurred in December 1968 when a Viscount, a 707, three Comets, two Caravelles and a leased VC10 were reduced to scrap value by Israeli commandos. During other periods of strife, MEA has been forced to vacate its headquarters to operate on a temporary basis in Cyprus. Despite these frustrating setbacks, the airline has continued to expand its coverage with routes to the Middle East, Africa, Europe and North America.

FLEET:

Airbus A310-203: PH-AGC, PH-AGE, PH-AGF
Airbus A310-304: D-APOL, D-APOP
Boeing 707-3B4C: OD-AFD, OD-AFE
Boeing 707-323B: OD-AHF
Boeing 707-323C: OD-AHC, OD-AHD, OD-AHE
Boeing 707-347C: OD-AGU, OD-AGV
Boeing 747-2B4B: N202AE, N203AE, N204AE

UK airport served: Heathrow.

Monarch Airlines (ZB/MOM) — United Kingdom
Luton Airport, Bedfordshire   Tel: (01582) 400000

Monarch was formed in 1967, with operations starting with two Britannias in April 1968. At first all services were flown from the carrier's base at Luton, but as the airline grew, so out-stations were set up at Gatwick and Manchester. Monarch was not only the first UK operator to employ the Boeing 720, but 12 years later in 1983 it also became the first independent to put the Boeing 757 into service. The airline later played a part in the founding of EuroBerlin by supplying and operating six Boeing 737-300s at a time when Lufthansa was not allowed to serve the nation's original capital. Unlike other holiday airlines, Monarch has continued to operate scheduled leisure services from Luton to a number of Spanish destinations, while its charter flights now take the fleet to Africa, across the Atlantic and to the Far East.

FLEET:

Airbus A300-605R: G-MAJS, G-MONR, G-MONS, G-OJMR

Above: **G-MONZ — Airbus A320-212 of Monarch Airlines.**

Airbus A320-212: G-MONW, G-MONX, G-MONY, G-MONZ, G-MPCD, G-OZBA, G-OZBB

Boeing 737-3Y0: G-BWJA

Boeing 737-33A: G-MONV

Boeing 757-2T7: G-DAJB, G-MONB, G-MOND, G-MONE, G-MONJ, G-MONK

Boeing 757-28A: G-MCKE

Douglas DC-10-30: G-DMCA

UK airports served: Birmingham, East Midlands, Gatwick, Glasgow, Liverpool, Luton, Manchester, Newcastle, Stansted and Teesside.

Nigeria Airways (WT/NGA)   Nigeria
PO Box 1024, Airways House, Ikeja, Lagos   Tel: (91) 90 08 10

Operations began in 1958 with the airline taking over the services formerly offered by West African Airways. By 1961 the company was wholly owned by the government which encouraged the airline to steadily expand its activities, particularly the domestic routes which were soon carrying more traffic than those of any other African carrier. Four Airbus A310s were ordered for delivery in 1984, the extra capacity intended for the over-subscribed domestic and regional sectors, but in the event the type was often employed on the international services. Financial difficulties have handicapped the airline in the past few years, resulting in the suspension of some routes and a reduction in the workforce.

FLEET:

Airbus A310-222: 5N-AUE, 5N-AUF, 5N-AUG, 5N-AUH

Douglas DC-10-30: 5N-ANN

Also operated is a Boeing 737.

UK airport served: Heathrow.

Northwest Airlines (NW/NWA) USA
Minneapolis/St Paul International Airport,
St Paul, Mn 55111 Tel: (612) 726 21 11

When founded in 1926 the airline was known as Northwest Airways, but changed its name to Northwest Orient in 1934, which it then retained until the mid-1980s when Orient was dropped. Prior to the war, the airline was kept busy with passenger schedules and mail flights, but after the US became involved with the Japanese in 1941, Northwest provided many services for the military from its operating base in Alaska. Its route network has steadily expanded to cover all parts of the US, together with transpacific and transatlantic schedules. To further consolidate its position, the company absorbed Republic Airlines in 1986 and has since established Northwest Air Link to feed its major hubs.

Above: **N144JC — Douglas DC-10-40 of Northwest Airlines.**

FLEET:

Boeing 747-212B: N641NW, N642NW

Boeing 747-227B: N633US, N634US, N635US

Boeing 747-251F: N616US, N617US, N618US, N619US, N629US, N639US, N640US

Boeing 747-251B: N611US, N612US, N613US, N614US, N615US, N622US, N623US, N624US, N625US, N626US, N627US, N628US, N631US, N632US, N636US, N637US, N638US

Boeing 747-2J9F: N630US

Boeing 747-451: N661US, N662US, N663US, N664US, N665US, N666US, N667US, N668US, N669US, N670US

Douglas DC-10-30: N211NW, N220NW, N221NW, N223NW, N224NW, N225NW, N226NW, N227NW, N228NW, N229NW, N230NW, N232NW, N233NW,

N234NW, N235NW

Douglas DC-10-40: N133JC, N141US, N144JC, N145US, N146US, N147US, N148US, N149US, N150US, N151US, N152US, N153US, N154US, N155US, N156US,N157US, N158US, N159US, N160US, N161US, N162US

Also operated are Airbus A320s, Boeing 727/757s, DC-9s and MD80s.

UK airport served: Gatwick.

Oasis International Airlines (OB/AAN)　　Spain
Calle Gobelas 17, Urbanizacion La Florida,
E-28023 Madrid　　　　　　　　　　　　　**Tel: (1) 372 85 86**

Above: **EC-FVC — McD Douglas MD83 of Oasis International Airlines.**

Formed in 1986, the airline was originally known as Andalusair. A wide range of IT charter flights are operated from mainland Spain and the Canary Islands to the UK and central Europe. Long-haul flights are also provided to Mexico.

FLEET:

Airbus A310-304: EC-

Airbus A310-324: EC-FXB

McD Douglas MD83: EC-FVB, EC-FVC

UK airports served: Birmingham, Glasgow, Manchester, Newcastle and Prestwick.

Olympic Airways (OA/OAL)　　Greece
96 Syngrou Avenue, Athens 11741　　　　**Tel: (1) 926 91 11**

After World War 2 three Greek airlines struggled to survive independently without a great deal of success. Finally they were merged to form TAE-Greek Airlines, but this did little better, so was taken over by the government in 1955. Two years later Aristotle Onassis bought the carrier and renamed it Olympic

Airways. Under his control the company quickly expanded, helped in no small way by the introduction of Comets on to the Athens–London route. As the network grew, so the fleet increased with Boeing 707s inaugurating a New York service in 1966. However, by 1974 Olympic was in serious financial trouble. Heavy losses forced Onassis to relinquish his 50-year agreement to run the company, whereupon the airline was grounded pending reorganisation and an injection of capital. Once again the Greek government mounted a rescue mission and this time Olympic has remained wholly owned by the state.

FLEET:

Airbus A300B4-103: SX-BED, SX-BEE, SX-BEF, SX-BEG, SX-BEH, SX-BEI

Airbus A300-605R: SX-BEK, SX-BEL

Boeing 727-230: SX-CBG, SX-CBH, SX-CBI

Boeing 727-284: SX-CBC, SX-CBD

Boeing 737-284: SX-BCA, SX-BCB, SX-BCC, SX-BCD, SX-BCE, SX-BCF, SX-BCG, SX-BCH, SX-BCI, SX-BCK, SX-BCL

Boeing 737-484: SX-BKA, SX-BKB, SX-BKC, SX-BKD, SX-BKE, SX-BKF, SX-BKG

Boeing 747-212B: SX-OAC, SX-OAD, SX-OAE

Boeing 747-284B: SX-OAB

UK airport served: Heathrow.

Onur Air (8Q/OHY)   Turkey
Senlikkoy Mahallesi 3, Florya, Istanbul 34810   Tel: (212) 663 23 00

Founded in 1992, Onur Air operates IT charters between Turkey and European points including the UK.

FLEET:

Airbus A300B4-103: TC-ONK, TC-ONL

Airbus A320-211: TC-ONC, TC-OND

Airbus A320-212: TC-ONE

Airbus A320-231: TC-ONF, TC-ONG

Airbus A321-131: TC-ONH, TC-ONI, TC-ONJ

UK airports served: Birmingham, East Midlands, Gatwick, Glasgow, Manchester, Newcastle and Stansted.

Pakistan International Airlines (PK/PIA)   Pakistan
PIA Building, Karachi Airport, Karachi   Tel: (21) 457 20 11

The company was founded in 1954 as the country's national carrier some time after the partitioning of India. Initially it was intended that PIA would concentrate on international activities, but after the merger with Orient Airlines in 1955 the coverage was extended to include both domestic and regional operations. In 1960 PIA became the first airline in Asia to operate jet equipment when Boeing 707s were introduced to the London route. The scheduled network now extends to Europe, North America, Africa and the Far East, employing A310s and Boeing 747s.

FLEET:

Airbus A310-308: AP-BDZ, AP-BEB, AP-BEC, AP-BEG, AP-BEQ, AP-BEU	
Boeing 747-217B: AP-BCL, AP-BCM, AP-BCN, AP-BCO	
Boeing 747-240B: AP-BAK, AP-BAT	
Boeing 747-282B: AP-AYV, AP-AYW	
Also operated are Airbus A300s, Boeing 737s and Friendships.	

UK airports served: Heathrow and Manchester.

Pegasus Airlines (PGT)   Turkey
34800 Istayon Caddesi, Yesilyurt, Istanbul   Tel: (212) 663 29 31

When Pegasus was formed in 1989 it was owned by Aer Lingus, but the Irish carrier sold its holding to Yapi in 1994. The airline operates IT charters to airports in Finland, France, Germany, Israel, the Netherlands, Norway and the UK from a number of hubs in Turkey.

FLEET:

Boeing 737-4Q8: TC-AFA, TC-AFM	
Boeing 737-4Y0: TC-AFK, TC-AFZ, TC-	

UK airports served: Cardiff, Glasgow, Manchester, Newcastle and Prestwick.

Philippine Airlines (PR/PAL)   Philippines
PO Box 954, Manila   Tel: (2) 818 01 11

Philippine Airlines was formed in February 1941 to take over from the bankrupt Philippine Air Transport. It proved not to be the best time for such a venture because within a year or so the Japanese had arrived, destroying the carrier's fleet during the course of their triumphant advance. A fresh start was made in 1946 using ex-military DC-3s for some domestic services, but the following year saw the inauguration of a transpacific route to San Francisco. Europe came next, with London at the end of a route which linked Manila with Bangkok, Calcutta, Karachi, Cairo, Rome and Madrid. Unfortunately, the success was not

Below: **N207AE — Boeing 747-211B of Philippine Airlines.**

to last. Falling loads and loss of traffic rights brought the suspension of almost all overseas services in 1954, the exception being Hong Kong. It was 1962 before the airline resumed its international links which now total 34. The airline is no longer wholly owned by the government, although the latter still has a 33% share. A consortium of local banking investors known as PR Holdings acquired 67% of the company in 1992.

FLEET:

Boeing 747-211B: N207AE, N208AE	
Boeing 747-212B: RP-C5746	
Boeing 747-283B: EI-BTS, EI-BZA	
Boeing 747-2F6B: N741PR, N742PR, N743PR, N744PR	
Boeing 747-469: N754PR	
Boeing 747-4F6: N751PR, N752PR, N753PR	
Also operated are Airbus A300s, Boeing 737s, DC-10s and Fokker 50s.	

UK airport served: Gatwick.

Polar Air Cargo (PO/PAC)   USA
100 Oceangate, 15th Floor, Long Beach, CA 90802   Tel: (310) 436 74 71

The airline was formed in 1993 with two 747s available for worldwide freight work. Polar received flag carrier certification in May 1995 and now provides international, regional and domestic freight services, both scheduled and charter.

FLEET:

Boeing 747-121F: N830FT, N831FT, N832FT	
Boeing 747-122F: N850FT, N851FT, N852FT, N853FT, N854FT	
Boeing 747-123F: N858FT, N859FT	
Boeing 747-124F: N855FT	
Boeing 747-132F: N857FT, N856FT	

UK airports served: Heathrow and Prestwick.

Portugalia (NI/PGA)   Portugal
Avenida Gago Coutinho 88, P-1700 Lisboa   Tel: (1) 848 66 93

The carrier was formed on 25 July 1989 with operations starting a year later. Portugalia provides a number of scheduled services from Lisbon to cities in Belgium, France, Germany, Italy and Spain. It also flies IT charter services to the Portuguese holiday areas.

FLEET:

Fokker 100: CS-TPA, CS-TPB, CS-TPC, CS-TPD, CS-TPE, CS-TPF, CS-	

UK airport served: Manchester.

Premiair (DK/VKG)   Denmark
Hangar 276, Copenhagen Airport South,
Dragoer DK-2791   Tel: (32) 45 45 00

Above: **OY-CNT — Douglas DC-10-10 of Premiair.**

The airline was created by the merger of Conair and Scanair on 1 January 1994.
Both carriers operated IT charters from Scandinavia, a duty since continued by
the combined force.

FLEET:
Airbus A300B4-120: OY-CNA, OY-CNK, OY-CNL
Airbus A320-231: OY-CND, OY-CNE, OY-CNF, OY-CNG, OY-CNH, OY-CNI
Douglas DC-10-10: OY-CNS, OY-CNT, OY-CNU, OY-CNY, OY-CNZ, SE-DHZ

UK airports served: Birmingham, Manchester and Stansted.

Proteus Air System (YS/PRB)   France
Aéroport Dijon-Bourgogne, F-21600 Longvic   Tel: (80) 63 13 63

Below: **F-GKST — Beech 1900-1 of Proteus Air System.**

Founded in 1986 as an air-taxi operator, Proteus now operates a twice-daily schedule to Stansted from Lille, plus a once-daily trip from its home base at Dijon. It also operates French domestic services for Air Inter Europe.

FLEET:

Beech B200 Super King Air: F-GPAS

Beech 1900-1: F-GKST

Dornier Do328-110: F-GNBS, F-GNPA

UK airport served: Stansted.

Qantas (QF/QFA)   Australia
PO Box 489, International Square, Sydney   Tel: (2) 691 36 36

Qantas has the distinction of being one of the world's oldest airlines having been formed in 1920 as the Queensland and Northern Territories Aerial Service. Domestic services began in 1922, while the airline pioneered a Brisbane–Singapore link in 1934, which in due course completed the London–Australia route. At this point the company changed its name to Qantas Empire Airways, which signified its association with Imperial Airways on this particular operation. In fact, it was not until 1967 that 'Empire' was dropped from the title. During 1953 Qantas took over British Commonwealth Pacific Airlines which gave it access to America. The domestic carrier, Australian Airlines, was acquired in 1992, but in the same year British Airways was successful in gaining a 25% share of Qantas.

FLEET:

Boeing 747-438: VH-OJA, VH-OJB, VH-OJC, VH-OJD, VH-OJE, VH-OJF, VH-OJG, VH-OJH, VH-OJI, VH-OJJ, VH-OJK, VH-OJL, VH-OJM, VH-OJN, VH-OJO, VH-OJP, VH-OJQ, VH-OJR

Also operated are Airbus A300, Boeing 737/767 and 747-200/300/SP.

UK airport served: Heathrow.

Qatar Airways (Q7/QTR)   Qatar
PO Box 22550, Almana Tower, Airport Road, Doha   Tel: 43 07 07

The airline started operations in January 1944 with scheduled services mainly to the Middle and Far East, but Europe is included with a route to London.

FLEET:

Boeing 747SP-27: A7-ABM

Boeing 747-SR-81: A7-ABK, A7-ABL

UK airport served: Gatwick.

Regional Airlines (VM/AVD) — France
Nantes Atlantiques Aéroport, Bouguenais 44340   Tel: (40) 84 81 38

Above: **F-GMVM — BAe Jetstream 32 of Regional Airlines.** *A. S. Wright*

A merger between Air Vendee and Airlec was responsible for the creation of this French regional carrier. It operates some 110 flights on a daily basis, visiting 30 cities located in eight countries.

FLEET:

Aérospatiale ATR42-300: F-GEQJ, F-GREG

BAe Jetstream 32: F-GMVH, F-GMVI, F-GMVJ, F-GMVK, F-GMVL, F-GMVM, F-GMVN, F-GMVO, F-GMVP

Embraer EMB-145: F-GMVE, F-GMVF, F-GMVG

SAAB SF340B: F-GHVS, F-GHVT, F-GHVU, F-GMVV, F-GMVX, F-GMVY, F-GMVZ

SAAB 2000: F-GMVB, F-GMVC, F-GMVD, F-GMVR

UK airports served: None regularly.

Rich International Airways (JN/RIA) — USA
PO Box 522067, Miami, FL 33152   Tel: (305) 871 51 13

The airline began operations in 1970 to operate worldwide commercial and military charter services. Subsequently it has added schedules to its activities from a number of hubs in the US.

FLEET:

Douglas DC-8-62: N772CA, N1805, N8974U

Douglas DC-8-63: N4935C

L1011-385 TriStar 1: N300AW, N302MB, N303EA, N304EA, N313EA, N319EA

L1011-385 TriStar 50: N762BE, N764BE, N765BE, N766BE

L1011-385 TriStar 200: N306GB

UK airports served: Gatwick, Glasgow, Manchester and Stansted.

Royal Air Maroc (AT/RAM) — Morocco
Anfa Airport, Casablanca — Tel: (3) 91 20 00

Two airlines were formed in Morocco after World War 2 which used ex-military equipment to serve destinations such as Paris, Geneva and Frankfurt. The two companies merged in 1953 which resulted in the Compagnie Cherifienne de Transport Aérien (CCTA) taking over the combined operation. It assumed the present title in June 1957 soon after the country's independence and was therefore designated the national carrier. In addition to European, domestic and regional services, the airline also visits both North and South America.

FLEET:

Boeing 727-2B6: CN-RMP, CN-RMQ, CN-RMR

Boeing 737-2B6: CN-RMI, CN-RMJ, CN-RMK, CN-RML, CN-RMM, CN-RMN

Boeing 737-4B6: CN-RMF, CN-RMG, CN-RMX, CN-RNA, CN-RNC, CN-RND, CN-RNE, CN-RNF

Boeing 737-5B6: CN-RMV, CN-RMW, CN-RMY, CN-RNB, CN-RNG, CN-RNH

Boeing 747-2B6B: CN-RME

Boeing 747-428: CN-RGA

Boeing 757-2B6: CN-RMT, CN-RMZ

UK airport served: Heathrow.

Royal Airlines (QN/ROY) — Canada
6700 Côte de Liesse, Suite 503, Montreal — Tel: (514) 739 70 00

Royal began operations in April 1992 with a series of international charter services including regular transatlantic sorties to France and the UK. During the northern winter season the airline offers routes to the Caribbean, Florida, Mexico and South America.

FLEET:

L1011-385 TriStar 100: C-FTNI, C-FTNK

Also operated are Boeing 727s.

UK airport served: Glasgow.

Royal Brunei Airlines (BI/RBA)   Brunei
PO Box 737, Bandar Seri Begawan 1907   Tel: (2) 24 05 00

Founded in November 1974, the government-owned national carrier of Brunei operates scheduled and charter services to Europe, the Middle and Far East.

FLEET:

Airbus A340-211: V8-BKH

Boeing 757-2M6: V8-RBA, V8-RBB

Boeing 767-33AER: V8-RBE, V8-RBF, V8-RBG, V8-RBH, V8-RBJ, V8-RBK, V8-RBL

UK airport served: Heathrow.

Royal Jordanian Airlines (RJ/RJA)   Jordan
PO Boz 302, Amman   Tel: (6) 67 91 78

A royal decree in December 1963 specified that the carrier should be formed to take over from Jordan Airways, which only two years earlier had replaced Air Jordan. At first only neighbouring countries were served, but gradually international routes were added until most of the major European cities were included in the network.

FLEET:

Airbus A310-203: 7T-VJE, 7T-VJF

Airbus A310-304: F-ODVF, F-ODVG, F-ODVH, F-ODVI

Airbus A320-211: F-OGYA, F-OGYB, F-OGYC

Boeing 707-365C: JY-AJM

Boeing 707-384C: JY-AJK

Boeing 707-3J6C: JY-AJN, JY-AJO

L1011-385 TriStar 500: JY-AGA, JY-AGB, JY-AGC, JY-AGD, JY-AGE, JY-AGF

UK airports served: Heathrow, Manchester and Stansted.

Below: **F-OGYA — Airbus A320-211 of Royal Jordanian Airlines.**

Royal Nepal Airlines (RA/RNA)
Nepal
PO Box 401, RNAC Building, Kanti Path,
Kathmandu

Tel: (1) 22 22 68

The airline was formed by the government in 1958 to take over all the
international routes between Nepal and India. It now links Kathmandu with 37
domestic points in addition to services to Europe.

FLEET:

Airbus A310-304: D-APON

Boeing 757-2F8: 9N-ACA, 9N-ACB

UK airport served: Gatwick.

Ryanair (FR/RYR)
Eire
Dublin Airport, Co Dublin

Tel: (1) 844 44 00

When operations started in 1985, a single weekday service between Waterford
and Gatwick was flown with a 15-seat Bandeirante. From that small beginning
the company quickly expanded with more routes and aircraft providing
low-cost schedules at high frequencies. A number of One-Elevens joined the
fleet, while Luton became the chosen UK gateway at first, although later the
majority of the activities were transferred to Stansted. In 1994 the airline
replaced its fleet with a number of ex-Britannia Boeing 737-200s, with more of
the type added in 1995, this time ex-Transavia.

FLEET:

Boeing 737-204ADV: EI-CJC, EI-CJD, EI-CJE, EI-CJF, EI-CJG, EI-CJH

Boeing 737-2E7ADV: EI-CJI

Boeing 737-2K2ADV: EI-CKP, EI-CKQ, EI-CKR

Boeing 737-2T5ADV: EI-CKS

UK airports served: Birmingham, Bournemouth, Cardiff, Gatwick,
Leeds/Bradford, Liverpool, Luton, Manchester, Prestwick and Stansted.

Ryanair UK (FR/CYR)
United Kingdom
Room 60, Terminal Building, Stansted Airport

Tel: (01279) 663082

Set up in 1995 by Ryanair with the intention of providing UK domestic services,
the airline's first link was between Stansted and Prestwick. Since this was
deemed an extension of the parent company's Dublin-Prestwick schedule, as a
foreign carrier only 50% of the seats could be offered initially. When the low
fare services began in October 1995 it was intended that GB Airways'
Operator's Certificate and aircraft would be used, but in fact Ryanair UK has
access to the Irish company's Boeing 737-200s which are flown without any
identifying UK titles. Although the airline planned to expand its route network
into Europe, by mid-1996 the Scottish schedule remained its only service, mainly
due to the non-availability of suitable 737-200s to provided the extra capacity.

FLEET:

See Ryanair

UK airports served: Prestwick and Stansted.

SABENA (SN/SAB) — Belgium
2 Avenue E. Mounierlaan, Brussels B-1200   Tel: (2) 723 43 01

The Belgian flag carrier came into being on 23 May 1923 following some reorganisation of the existing companies. It slowly expanded the route network radiating from Brussels, but at the same time provided services in the Congo. During World War 2 all activities in Belgium were suspended, but the African operation was able to continue throughout the period.

SABENA resumed its work quickly after the end of hostilities, so once suitable equipment was available, it was possible for the carrier to begin transatlantic flights to America in 1947. Nowadays the airline has a comprehensive network which includes routes to Asia, Africa, North America and numerous European cities. Air France possesses a 33% share in the Belgian company, but an agreement reached in March 1995 resulted in Swissair acquiring a 49% stake.

FLEET:

Airbus A310-222: OO-SCA, OO-SCB

Airbus A310-322: OO-SCC

Airbus A340-211: OO-SCW, OO-SCX

Boeing 737-229: OO-SDA, OO-SDD, OO-SDE, OO-SDF, OO-SDG, OO-SDJ, OO-SDK, OO-SDL, OO-SDM, OO-SDN, OO-SDO, OO-SDP, OO-SDR

Below: **PH-SDJ — DHC-8-311A Dash Eight of SABENA/Schreiner Airways.**

| Boeing 737-329: | OO-SDV, OO-SDW, OO-SDX, OO-SDY, OO-SYA, OO-SYB |

Boeing 737-329: OO-SDV, OO-SDW, OO-SDX, OO-SDY, OO-SYA, OO-SYB

Boeing 737-429: OO-SYC, OO-SYD, OO-SYF

Boeing 737-529: OO-SYE, OO-SYG, OO-SYH, OO-SYI, OO-SYJ, OO-SYK

Boeing 747-329: OO-SGC, OO-SGD

DHC-8-311A Dash Eight: PH-SDI, PH-SDJ, PH-SDM, PH-SDP, PH-SDR

Douglas DC-10-30: OO-SLG, OO-SLH

UK airports served: Bristol, Edinburgh, Glasgow, Heathrow, Leeds/Bradford, London City, Manchester and Newcastle. (Some services operated by DAT and Schreiner aircraft.)

Sabre Airways (SBE)   United Kingdom
12 The Merlin Centre, County Oak Way, Crawley, West Sussex   Tel: (01293) 410727

The airline was set up in December 1994 to take over some of the commitments of the defunct Ambassador Airways. Two Boeing 737-200s were acquired for IT operations starting on 17 December initially using AirFoyle's Operator's Certificate until Sabre gained its own in December 1995.

FLEET:

Boeing 727-2D3: G-BPND

Boeing 737-204ADV: G-SBEA, G-SBEB

Boeing 727-276: G-BNNI

Above: **G-SBEA — Boeing 737-204ADV of Sabre Airways.**

UK airports served: Gatwick, Liverpool, Luton, Manchester and Newcastle.

Above: **SE-DME — McD Douglas MD81 of SAS.**

Each of the three Scandinavian countries had its own national airline from the very early days of air transport: Danish Air Lines (DDL) was formed in 1918, Swedish Air Lines (ABA) in 1924 and finally Norwegian Air Lines (DNL) came into being in 1927. After World War 2, the expected growth of international services brought about the creation of SAS in 1946. It was intended that this new airline would be responsible for the three countries' combined long-haul services, leaving the European operations with the individual carriers. This was the case until February 1951 when the entire network came under SAS's control.

Subsequently the airline has grown considerably and now serves 101 destinations in 34 countries. It has often pioneered new routes, probably the most notable being a Far East service in 1949 and the flights over the North Pole to reach the west coast of America and Tokyo, via Anchorage in Alaska, in 1954 and 1957 respectively.

The operations of the Swedish carrier Linjeflyg were absorbed into SAS in 1993, which also has a financial holding in the Airlines of Britain Group and Spanair. Domestic and regional services are operated by SAS Commuter which has Swedair as a subsidiary company.

FLEET:

Boeing 767-383ER: LN-RCD, LN-RCE, LN-RCG, LN-RCH, LN-RCI, LN-RCK, LN-RCL, OY-KDH, OY-KDL, OY-KDM, OY-KDN, OY-KDO, SE-DOC

Boeing 767-3Y0ER: SE-DKY

Douglas DC-9-41: LN-RLA, LN-RLH, LN-RLN, LN-RLP, LN-RLS, LN-RLT, LN-RLZ, OY-KGL, OY-KGM, OY-KGN, OY-KGO, OY-KGP, OY-KGR, OY-KGS, SE-DAR, SE-DAS, SE-DAU, SE-DAW, SE-DAX, SE-DBM, SE-DDP, SE-DDR, SE-DDS, SE-DDT

F28 Fellowship 1000: SE-DGA, SE-DGB, SE-DBC

F28 Fellowship 4000: SE-DGE, SE-DGF, SE-DGG, SE-DGH, SE-DGI, SE-DGK, SE-DGL, SE-DGM, SE-DGN, SE-DGO, SE-DGP, SE-DGR, SE-DGS, SE-DGT, SE-DGU, SE-DGX

Fokker 50: LN-RNB, LN-RNC, LN-RND, LN-RNE, LN-RNF, LN-RNG, LN-RNH, OY-KAE, OY-KAF, OY-KAG, OY-KAH, OY-KAI, OY-KAK, SE-LFA, SE-LFB, SE-LFC, SE-LFK, SE-LFN, SE-LFO, SE-LFP, SE-LFR, SE-LFS

McD Douglas MD81: LN-RMA, LN-RMJ, LN-RML, LN-RMM, LN-RMO, LN-RMR, LN-RMS, LN-RMT, OY-KGY, OY-KGZ, OY-KHC, OY-KHG, OY-KHK, OY-KHL, OY-KHM, OY-KHN, OY-KHP, OY-KHR, OY-KIG, OY-KIH, OY-KII, OY-KIK, SE-DFR, SE-DFY, SE-DIA, SE-DII, SE-DIL, SE-DIN, SE-DIR, SE-DIS, SE-DIX, SE-DIY, SE-DMB, SE-DMD, SE-DME,SE-DMU, SE-DMX, SE-DMY, SE-DMZ

McD Douglas MD82: LN-RLE, LN-RLF, LN-RLG, LN-RLR, LN-RMD, LN-RMN, OY-KHT, SE-DFS, SE-DFT, SE-DIK, SE-DIZ

McD Douglas MD83: LN-RMF, SE-DPH, SE-DPI

McD Douglas MD87: LN-RMG, LN-RMH, LN-RMK, LN-RMP, LN-RMU, OY-KHF, OY-KHI, OY-KHU, OY-KHW, SE-DIB, SE-DIC, SE-DIF, SE-DIH, SE-DIP, SE-DIU, SE-DMA

McD Douglas MD90: SE-DMF, SE-DMG, LN-ROA, LN-ROB, OY-KIL, OY-KIM

UK airports served: Aberdeen, Edinburgh, Heathrow, Manchester and Newcastle.

Saudia-Saudi Arabian Airlines (SV/SVA)

Saudi Arabia

PO Box 620, Jeddah 21231 — Tel: (2) 686 00 00

Saudia was created in 1945 in an attempt to improve the country's communications. Charters and mail runs were carried out by DC-3s, which also undertook scheduled services from 1947. Until 1962 there were few attempts made to leave the boundaries of the Arab countries, but with the delivery of a pair of Boeing 720s, the airline was tempted to venture further afield. Bombay, Karachi and Istanbul were added to the carrier's network, but it was May 1967 before a route to any European city was offered, the first taking in Geneva, Frankfurt and London. Eventually Saudia became a wide-body operator with a large fleet of TriStars, Boeing 747s and Airbus A300s. The airline is now the largest in the Middle East, with services to Europe, Asia, Africa, the Middle and Far East and the US.

FLEET:

Airbus A300-620: HZ-AJA, HZ-AJB, HZ-AJC, HZ-AJD, HZ-AJE, HZ-AJF, HZ-AJG, HZ-AJH, HZ-AJI, HZ-AJJ, HZ-AJK

Boeing 747-168B: HZ-AIA, HZ-AIB, HZ-AIC, HZ-AID, HZ-AIE, HZ-AIG, HZ-AIH, HZ-AII

Boeing 747-368: HZ-AIL, HZ-AIM, HZ-AIN, HZ-AIO, HZ-AIP, HZ-AIQ, HZ-AIR, HZ-AIS, HZ-AIT

Boeing 747-468: HZ-AIV

Boeing 747-268F: HZ-AIU

Boeing 747SP-68: HZ-AIF

L1011-385 TriStar 200: HZ-AHA, HZ-AHB, HZ-AHC, HZ-AHD, HZ-AHE, HZ-AHF, HZ-AHG, HZ-AHH, HZ-AHI, HZ-AHJ, HZ-AHL, HZ-AHM, HZ-AHN, HZ-AHO, HZ-AHP, HZ-AHQ, HZ-AHR

UK airport served: Heathrow.

Singapore Airlines (SQ/SIA) — Singapore
PO Box 501, Singapore 9181   Tel: 542 33 33

When Malaysia and Singapore parted company in 1967, Malaysian Airways changed its name to Malaysian Singapore Airlines to reflect its joint ownership. The scheme worked reasonably well until disagreement over expansion plans forced a split. Singapore Airlines was formed in January 1972, its aim being to concentrate on international services. On the other hand, Malaysian Airline System, as the second carrier was now known, intended to place more emphasis on domestic route development. SIA has since extended its network using a large fleet of young, modern airliners.

FLEET:

Boeing 747-212F: 9V-SKQ

Boeing 747-312: 9V-SKA, 9V-SKD, 9V-SKM, 9V-SKN, 9V-SKP, N117KC, N121KG, N122KH, N123KJ, N124KK, N125KL

Boeing 747-412: 9V-SMA, 9V-SMB, 9V-SMC, 9V-SMD, 9V-SME, 9V-SMF, 9V-SMG, 9V-SMH, 9V-SMI, 9V-SMJ, 9V-SMK, 9V-SML, 9V-AMM, 9V-AMN, 9V-SMO, 9V-SMP, 9V-SMQ, 9V-SMR, 9V-SMS, 9V-SMT, 9V-SMU, 9V-SMV, 9V-SMW, 9V-SMY, 9V-SMZ, 9V-SPA, 9V-SPB, 9V-SPC, 9V-SPD, 9V-SPE, 9V-SPF, 9V-SPG, 9V-SPH, 9V-SPI, 9V-SPJ, 9V-SPK, 9V-SPL

Boeing 747-412F: 9V-SFA, 9V-SFB, 9V-SFC, 9V-SFD, 9V-SFE, 9V-SFF

Also operated are Airbus A310 and Airbus A340

UK airports served: Heathrow and Manchester.

Below: **9V-SMS — Boeing 747-412 of Singapore Airlines.**

Sobelair (SLR)
131 Avenue Frans Courtens, B-1030 Brussels

Belgium
Tel: (2) 247 52 11

Sobelair was founded in July 1946, much of its work involving charters between Belgium and the Congo. It also provided domestic services within the African colony which were arranged to offer connections with the trunk schedules flown by SABENA. The latter acquired a majority interest in the company in 1948, an association which has since continued. When activities in the Congo ended with the state's independence in 1962, Sobelair began to concentrate on IT charters, although scheduled services are flown for its parent when required.

FLEET:

Boeing 737-229: OO-SBQ, OO-SBT	
Boeing 737-329: OO-SBZ	
Boeing 737-3M8: OO-SBX	
Boeing 737-46B: OO-SBJ	
Boeing 737-429: OO-SBM	
Boeing 737-4C9: LX-LGF	
Boeing 767-33AER: OO-SBY	
Boeing 767-328ER: OO-STF	

UK airports served: None regularly.

South African Airways (SA/SAA)
Airways Towers, PO Box 7778, Johannesburg 2000

South Africa
Tel: (11) 978 11 11

Above: ZS-SDG — **Airbus A300C4 of South African Airways.**

Union Airways was founded in 1929 in an attempt to improve communications in South Africa, becoming the national carrier in February 1934. A year or so later the airline absorbed South West African Airways as part of an expansion programme designed to further enlarge the domestic network.

SAA's first international route was introduced soon after the war, connecting the UK with Johannesburg after an inaugural flight on 10 November 1945. The service employed Yorks, DC-4s and Constellations, but in 1953 the airline became the first non-British carrier to employ jet airliners when it leased a pair of Comets from BOAC. Sadly it was a short interlude, it being 1960 before the airline was able to restart such services with a Boeing 707. November 1971 marked the introduction of wide-bodied equipment bringing the benefits of non-stop flights to London using the Boeing 747.

FLEET:

Airbus A300C4-203: ZS-SDG
Boeing 747-244B: ZS-SAL, ZS-SAM, ZS-SAN, ZS-SAO, ZS-SAP, ZS-SAR
Boeing 747-321: ZS-SAC, ZS-SAJ, ZS-SAZ
Boeing 747-344: ZS-SAT, ZS-SAU
Boeing 747-444: ZS-SAV, ZS-SAW, ZS-SAX, ZS-SAY
Boeing 747SP-44: ZS-SPB, ZS-SPC, ZS-SPE
Also operated are **Airbus A300B4/A320** and **Boeing 737.**

UK airports served: Heathrow and Stansted (cargo).

Southern Air Transport (SJ/SJM)   USA
PO Box 52-4093, Miami, Fl33152   Tel: (305) 871 63 92

Worldwide cargo services are provided by this carrier which was founded in 1947 to specialise in the movement of outsize feight. Subsequently the airline has become associated with Polar Air Cargo, which operates scheduled and charter services between the USA and China.

FLEET:

Boeing 747-212F: N745SJ
Boeing 747-246F: N740SJ, N741SJ
Boeing 747-249F: N742SJ
Douglas DC-8-71F: N872SJ
Douglas DC-8-73F: N874SJ, N875SJ
L100-20 Hercules: N522SJ
L100-30 Hercules: N901SJ, N905SJ, N906SJ, N907SJ, N908SJ, N909SJ, 910SJ, N912SJ, N916SJ, N918SJ, N919SJ, N920SJ, N921SJ, N923SJ

UK airports served: None regularly.

Spanair (JK/SPP)   Spain
PO Box 50066, E-07000, Palma de Mallorca   Tel: (71) 49 20 12

The Spanish company has operated charters to Europe from the Canary Islands and Mallorca since it began flying in March 1988. Long-haul services are also flown to destinations in North and South America with Boeing 767s.

FLEET:

Boeing 767-3Y0ER: EC-FCU, EC-FHA

McD Douglas MD83: EC-EIG, EC-FSY, EC-FTS, EC-FTT, EC-FTU, EC-FVR, EC-FXA, EC-FXI, EC-FXY, EC-FZC, EC-GAT, EC-GBA, EC-GCV, EC-GGV, EC-GHE

UK airports served: Aberdeen, Belfast, Birminghamn, Bournemouth, East Midlands, Edinburgh, Exeter, Gatwick, Glasgow, Humberside, Leeds/Bradford, Liverpool, Manchester, Newcastle and Norwich.

Sterling European Airways (NB/SNB)   Denmark
Copenhagen Airport, DK-2791, Dragoer   Tel: 32 45 45 45

Sterling Airways was originally formed in 1962 for the pupose of flying IT charters to the Mediterranean and Canary Islands. The enterprise proved very successful with a large fleet of DC-6s giving way to Caravelles and Boeing 727s in the 1970s. In the early 1990s the company joined with Transwede and Norway Airlines to create the Trans Nordic Group, but this scheme was unsuccessful in its intention to compete with SAS. Sterling dropped a plan to launch a scheduled service to Gatwick due to its financial problems which resulted in bankruptcy in September 1993. Three months later Sterling European was created to continue the operations, albeit on a much smaller scale. Services were therefore able to restart on 1 May 1994 using Boeing 727s.

FLEET:

Boeing 727-212: OY-SCC

Boeing 727-270: OY-SBI

Boeing 727-2B7: OY-SBN

Boeing 727-2J4: OY-SAU

Boeing 727-2K3: OY-SBO

Boeing 727-2M7: OY-SEZ

UK airports served: East Midlands, Gatwick, Manchester and Stansted.

Suckling Airways (CB/SAY)   United Kingdom
Cambridge Airport, Newmarket Road, Cambridge   (01223) 292525

Daily passenger scheduled services are operated between Cambridge, Manchester and Amsterdam, together with Luton–Waterford and Amsterdam links. The airline began operations in April 1986 from Ipswich airport, but problems with the grass field forced the carrier to move elsewhere. Suckling was the first UK operator of the Dornier Do228, a type it has flown throughout its successful career. A Dornier Do328 was added to the fleet in October 1995 specifically for the newly acquired Luton-Paris route. The company also added Norwich–Manchester and Norwich-Luton-Paris services in the spring of 1996.

FLEET:

Dornier Do228-200: G-BMMR

Dornier Do228-202K: G-BUXT, G-BVPT, G-BVTZ, G-BWEX

Above: **G-BWIR — Dornier Do328-100 of Suckling Airways.**

Dornier Do328-100: G-BWIR

UK airports served: Cambridge, Luton, Manchester, Norwich and Stansted.

Sudan Airways (SD/SUD)
PO Box 253, Khartoum

Sudan
Tel: (11) 47 953

The flag carrier was formed in 1946 to allow a network of domestic services to be introduced. By 1959, international sectors had been added, London being one of the destinations served by a single Viscount. A modernisation programme was started in 1962 with the arrival of three Friendships, followed by the airline's first jet type, two Comet 4Cs. The latter were purchased to provide increased frequency and capacity on the London run, both serving faithfully until replaced by a pair of Boeing 707s. A major upheaval within the airline took place in 1983 when the management was disbanded by Presidential order. An attempt was made to sell the company but little interest was shown. As part of the changes it was decided that the carrier would adopt the title Nile Air, but before this could take effect the instigator was removed from power in April 1985. As so often the case, the new leader cancelled all plans conceived by his predecessor, leaving Sudan Airways as a state-owned company.

FLEET:

Airbus A300-622:	F-ODTK
Airbus A310-304:	F-GKTD, F-OGQN
Boeing 707-3J8C:	ST-AFA, ST-AFB
Boeing 707-369C:	ST-AIX

Also operated are Airbus A320, Boeing 737 and Fokker 50.

UK airport served: Heathrow.

Sunway (SWW) — Turkey
Cumhuriyet Caddesi 211-5,
TR-80230 Elmadag-Istanbul
Tel: (212) 231 42 00

This carrier was launched in 1995 to operate IT charters with MD83s between Turkey and northern Europe. Although the title differs slightly from that of a Swedish company, both fleets carry the same livery.

FLEET:
McD Douglas MD83: TC-INA, TC-INB, TC-INC, TC-IND

UK airports served: Birmingham, Cardiff, East Midlands, Edinburgh, Glasgow, Humberside, Liverpool, Luton, Manchester, Newcastle, Stansted and Teesside.

Sunways Airlines (SWY) — Sweden
Sveijavagen 49, S-11359 Stockholm
Tel: (8) 457 46 11

The company was formed in 1994 to operate charter flights from Scandinavia to Turkey with two ex-Ambassador Boeing 757s.

FLEET:
Boeing 757-23A: SE-DSM
Boeing 757-236: SE-DSK, SE-DSL

UK airports served: None regularly.

Swissair (SR/SWR) — Switzerland
Postfach, CH-8058 Zürich
Tel: (1) 812 12 12

The merger of Balair and Ad Astra in 1931 was responsible for the founding of the Swiss Air Transport Co. Known as Swissair, the airline possessed 13 aircraft, but this number quickly increased as fast, modern types were introduced. One such machine was the 15-seat Curtiss Condor which required the services of a cabin attendant, thereby giving the Swiss carrier the distinction of becoming the first European company to employ such a person.

World War 2 ended most of Swissair's activities for six years, although a few flights continued to Rome and Barcelona for a time, but, surrounded by countries at war, flying an airliner away from the safety of its neutral airspace became increasingly risky. All services were therefore abandoned in 1943, remaining so until the restart in 1945. In 1949 a Geneva–New York schedule began, the first of steady expansion of both fleet and network. The airline has always possessed modern equipment and, together with Lufthansa, was the launch customer for the Airbus A310. It was also the first operator of the MD81 in September 1980, while in 1985 it opted for the new Fokker 100.

In 1995 both the A310 and the Dutch-built type began to leave the company, following the delivery of the A321s and an order for Avro RJ100s and A319s. All aircraft of up to 100-seat size were transferred to Crossair in 1995/96, while Swissair absorbed some of Balair/CTA fleet.

FLEET:

Airbus A310-322: HB-IPF, HB-IPG, HB-IPH, HB-IPI, HB-IPK	
Airbus A310-325: HB-IPL, HB-IPM, HB-IPN	
Airbus A319-112: HB-IPV, HB-IPW, HB-IPX, HB-IPY, HB-IPZ	
Airbus A320-214: HB-IJA, HB-IJB, HB-IJC, HB-IJD, HB-IJE, HB-IJF, HB-IJG, HB-IJH, HB-IJI, HB-IJK, HB-IJL, HB-IJM, HB-IJN, HB-IJO, HB-IJP, HB-IJQ, HB-IJR	
Airbus A321-111: HB-IOA, HB-IOB, HB-IOC, HB-IOD, HB-IOE, HB-IOF, HB-IOG, HB-IOH	
Boeing 747-357: HB-IGC, HB-IGD, HB-IGE, HB-IGF, HB-IGG	
McD Douglas MD81: HB-INA, HB-INB, HB-IND, HB-INH, HB-INI, HB-INM, HB-INN, HB-INO, HB-INP, HB-INS, HB-INT, HB-INU, HB-INX, HB-INY	
McD Douglas MD11: HB-IWA, HB-IWB, HB-IWC, HB-IWD, HB-IWE, HB-IWF, HB-IWG, HB-IWH, HB-IWI, HB-IWK, HB-IWL, HB-IWM, HB-IWN, HB-IWO, HB-IWP, HB-IWQ	

UK airports served: Heathrow and Manchester.

Syrian Arab Airlines (RB/SYR) — Syria
PO Box 417, Youssel El-Azmeh Square, Damascus — Tel: (11) 23 21 59

Syrian Airways was founded in December 1946 to join the increasing band of airlines belonging to the Arab nations. By 1958 Egypt and Syria were sufficiently friendly in a political sense for the latter's air transport system to become part of the United Arab Airlines. As could be expected from the unstable region involved, this state of unity did not last. Amidst turmoil and a series of pointless coups, Syria left the group for the government to set up its own carrier. As Syrian Arab Airlines, the company's network has since progressively spread from its homeland with routes radiating from Damascus to the Middle East, Europe, North Africa and Asia.

FLEET:

Boeing 727-269: YK-AGD, YK-AGE, YK-AGF	
Boeing 727-294: YK-AGA, YK-AGB, YK-AGC	
Boeing 747SP-94: YK-AHA, YK-AHB	
Tupolev Tu-134B-3: YK-AYA, YK-AYB, YK-AYC, YK-AYD, YK-AYE, YK-AYF	
Tupolev Tu-154M: YK-AIA, YK-AIB, YK-AIC	

UK airport served: Heathrow.

TAP-Air Portugal (TP/TAP) — Portugal
Edificio 25, Aeroporto de Lisboa, P-1704 Lisboa — Tel: (1) 841 50 00

On 19 September 1946 a DC-3 flight between Lisbon and Madrid launched the

Above: **CS-TEX — Airbus A310-304 of TAP Air Portugal.** *A. S. Wright*

career of the newly-founded Transportes Aereos Portugueses (TAP). Services to Africa were soon added, while European and domestic routes were steadily introduced. In 1953 the privately controlled company merged with the long-established Aero Portuguesa, one result being the inauguration of long-haul routes. Brazil was served during 1960 in partnership with Panair Do Brasil, with New York finding itself on the airline's map in 1966.

Nationalisation overtook the carrier in April 1975, by which time an all-jet fleet was operated to over 40 destinations in Europe, the Americas and Africa. Although scheduled services had always been TAP's main activity, a greater effort was made in the 1980s to secure a larger share of the charter market. There was a considerable increase in the airline's presence around the UK in 1984, prompting the setting up of a subsidiary, known as Air Atlantis, to handle the work. However, after a few years mounting losses hastened the end of this carrier in 1993.

FLEET:

Airbus A310-304: CS-TEH, CS-TEI, CS-TEJ, CS-TEW, CS-TEX
Airbus A320-211: CS-TNA, CS-TNB, CS-TNC, CS-TND, CS-TNE, CS-TNF
Airbus A340-312: CS-TOA, CS-TOB, CS-TOC, CS-TOD
Boeing 737-230: CS-TES
Boeing 737-282: CS-TEM, CS-TEN, CS-TEO, CS-TEP, CS-TEQ
Boeing 737-382: CS-TIB, CS-TIC, CS-TID, CS-TIE, CS-TIK, CS-TIL
Boeing 737-3K9: CS-TIG, CS-TIH
Boeing 737-33A: CS-TIN, CS-TIO
L1011-385 TriStar 500: CS-TEA, CS-TEB, CS-TEC, CS-TED, CS-TEE

UK airports served: Gatwick and Heathrow.

Tarom (RO/ROT)
Otopeni Airport, Bucharest

Romania
Tel: (1) 633 53 92

Tarom has been government controlled since it was established in 1954, offering scheduled services to major cities in Africa, the Middle and Far East, Europe and the US. The Romanian carrier was not dominated by Russian types in its fleet, probably due to the influence of the locally-built One-Eleven.

FLEET:

Airbus A310-325: YR-LCA, YR-LCB, YR-

BAC One-Eleven 487GK: YR-BCR

BAC One-Eleven 525FT: YR-BCI, YR-BCJ, YR-BCK, YR-BCL, YR-BCM, YR-BCN

Boeing 707-3K1C: YR-ABA, YR-ABC

Boeing 707-321C: YR-ABN

Boeing 737-38J: YR-BGA, YR-BGB, YR-BGC, YR-BGD, YR-BGE

Ilyushin IL-18D: YR-IMJ, YR-IML

Ilyushin IL-18V: YR-IMF, YR-IMG

Ilyushin IL-62M: YR-IRD, YR-IRE

RomBac One-Eleven 561RC: YR-BRA, YR-BRB, YR-BRC, YR-BRD, YR-BRF, YR-BRG

Tupolev Tu-154B: YR-TPB, YR-TPE, YR-TPF, YR-TPG, YR-TPK, YR-TPL

UK airport served: Heathrow.

Below: **YR-BCN — BAC One-Eleven 525FT of Tarom.**

Conceived as an air-taxi operator, Touraine Air Transport soon began scheduled services by starting a Tours–Lyon link in March 1969. As the company grew it swallowed a number of smaller carriers, until its size and activities indicated that a more appropriate name was necessary. The airline therefore became Transport Aérien Transrégional in 1984, a title carefully chosen to retain the familiar initials TAT. Later the present identity was adopted, again to reflect the company's role in the industry.

TAT was granted new routes following Air France's take-over of UTA in 1990, while in 1992 British Airways acquired a 49% holding in the company with an option to purchase the remaining shares by April 1997. The revitalised TAT set up a new network of routes in 1993 which stretch throughout Europe, the aircraft employed being painted in BA livery with an indication of TAT's involvement. A wide range of domestic services are also flown from Paris and Lyon.

FLEET:

Aérospatiale ATR42-312: F-GGLK, F-GIRC, F-GKNA, F-GKNB, F-GKNC, F-GKND

Aérospatiale ATR72-202: F-GKOA, F-GKOB, F-GKOC, F-GKOD

Boeing 737-204C: F-GGPB, F-GGPC

Boeing 737-210C: F-GGFI

Boeing 737-242C: F-GGPA

Boeing 737-248C: F-GGFJ

Boeing 737-3Y0: F-GLLD, F-GLLE

F27J Friendship: F-GBRU

FH227B Friendship: F-GCPT, F-GCPU, F-GCPX, F-GCPY

F28 Fellowship 1000: F-GBBR, F-GBBS, F-GBBT, F-GBBX, F-GECK, F-GIAI, F-GIMH, F-GNZB

F28 Fellowship 2000: F-GDUS, F-GDUT, F-GDUU, F-GDUV

F28 Fellowship 4000: F-GDFC, F-GDSK, F-GDUY

Fokker 100: F-GIOA, F-GIOG, F-GIOH, F-GIOI, F-GIOJ, F-GIOK, F-GMPG

UK airports served: Gatwick and Leeds/Bradford.

The airline was formed in 1988 as a part of the expanding TEA group, flying IT charters from its Basel base to the various holiday areas. It managed to survive the collapse of the parent company in 1991, in due course adopting the title of TEA Switzerland instead of TEA Basel.

Above: **HB-IIC — Boeing 737-3M8 of TEA Switzerland**

FLEET:

Boeing 737-3M8: HB-IIA, HB-IIB, HB-IIC

Boeing 737-3Q8: HB-IIE, HB-IIF, HB-IIG

Boeing 737-3Y0: HB-IID

UK airports served: None regularly.

Thai Airways International (TG/THA)　　Thailand
89 Vibhavadi Rangsit Super Highway,
PO Box 1075, Bangkok 10900　　　Tel: (2) 513 01 21

The airline grew from Thai Airways in December 1959 after an agreement was reached with SAS so that international services could be operated by the flag carrier. Mainly regional routes were flown at first, but more ambitious steps were taken in 1971 when Australia was included in the airline's coverage. European destinations were added in the following year, with 1980 bringing America into the network. SAS's interest in the company was sold to the Thai government in March 1977, thereby giving it complete control. The airline now flies to 51 destinations located in 36 countries throughout Asia, Australia, Europe, the Middle East and the US. In 1992 Thai International became partially privatised, although the state remained a major shareholder.

FLEET:

Boeing 747-3D7: HS-TGD, HS-TGE

Boeing 747-4D7: HS-TGH, HS-TGJ, HS-TGK, HS-TGL, HS-TGM, HS-TGN, HS-TGO, HS-TGP, HS-TGR, HS-TGT

McD Douglas MD11: HS-TMD, HS-TME, HS-TMF, HS-TMG

Also operated are Airbus A300B4/A300-622R/A310/A330, BAe 146 and Boeing 737/777.

UK airport served: Heathrow.

Titan was formed in 1988 to operate general passenger and freight charters. A proposal to operate a regular scheduled service between London City and Belfast with Short SD3-60s failed to materialise, but since that time the company has introduced the ATR42-300 and was due to become the first UK operator of the longer-range Series 500 variant in 1995. This was subsequently dropped in favour of another 300 on lease. The company was contracted to fly a short programme of charters to Jersey from Southend on behalf of tour operator Travelsmith during the spring of that year, while in 1996 a similar programme was operated from Kent International and Gloucestershire.

FLEET:

Aérospatiale ATR42-300: G-BUPS, G-ZAPJ	
BAe 146-200QC: G-ZAPK	
Short SD3-30: G-ZAPC	
Short SD3-60: G-ZAPD, G-ZAPG	

UK airports served: East Midlands, Gatwick, Gloucester, Jersey, Liverpool, Manston, Norwich, Southend and Stansted.

Above: **G-ZAPG — Short SD3-60 of Titan Airways.**

TNT International (NTR)　　　　United Kingdom
Archway House, 114-116 St Leonards Road,
Windsor　　　　　　　　　　　　　　Tel: (01753) 842168

Above: **EI-TNT — Boeing 727-281F of TNT Express Worldwide.**

As a part of the Australian TNT Group, TNT International operates scheduled and charter freight services with a particular emphasis on the overnight movement of parcels throughout Europe. Many of the flights are undertaken by carriers under contract to TNT, using Cologne as the central hub for the redistribution of the cargo.

FLEET:

BAe 146-200QT: D-ADEI, D-ANTJ, EC-ELT, EC-EPA, EC-FVY, EC-FZE, G-TNTA, G-TNTB, I-TNTC,

BAe 146-300QT: G-TJPM, G-TNTE, G-TNTG, G-TNTK, G-TNTL, G-TNTM, G-TNTR, EC-FFY

Boeing 727-227F: EI-PAK

Boeing 727-243F: EI-EWW

Boeing 727-281F: EI-SKY, EI-TNT

UK airports served: Belfast, Birmingham, Edinburgh, Liverpool, Manchester and Stansted.

Tower Air (FF/TOW)　　　　　　USA
Hangar 8, JFK International, Jamaica,
New York NY-11430　　　　　　　　　Tel: (718) 917 43 00

The airline was founded in 1982 to take over the services previously flown by the defunct Metro Airways. Long-haul charters to Europe and the Far East began with a small collection of elderly Boeing 747s which has gradually grown to keep pace with the carrier's expansion into the scheduled scene. Tower Air has received permission to operate a service between Chicago, New York and

Stansted, thereby providing the much-needed transatlantic link from London's third airport. This was expected to be launched for the summer programme of 1996, but was duly postponed following a delay in receiving the final approval from the two governments.

FLEET:

Boeing 747-121: N604FF, N609FF	
Boeing 747-121F: N613FF, N615FF, N617FF	
Boeing 747-124: N602FF	
Boeing 747-130: N603FF	
Boeing 747-131: N608FF	
Boeing 747-136: N606FF	
Boeing 747-143: N621FF	
Boeing 747-212B: N616FF, N618FF, N619FF, N620FF	
Boeing 747-238B: N607FF, N614FF	
Boeing 747-282B: N610FF, N611FF	

UK airports served: Gatwick and Stansted.

Trans Mediterranean Airways (TL/TMA)   Lebanon
PO Box 11-3018, Beirut International Airport   Tel: (1) 83 14 33

Cargo operations began with Avro Yorks in 1953, later adding scheduled services to its activities. Eventually, Boeing 707s replaced the DC-4s and DC-6s in use in the 1960s, their arrival enabling the carrier to provide a worldwide coverage. In common with Middle East Airlines, TMA suffered disruption due to the constant skirmishes around its headquarters at Beirut. Since it was not the safest of locations for staff and machines, the airline suspended operations for a period until the situation improved. Although services were later resumed, the financial losses had been increasing, bringing an end to the airline in mid-1996.

Trans World Airlines (TW/TWA)   USA
515, North 6th Street, St Louis, Mo   Tel: (314) 589 30 00

A series of take-overs and mergers finally resulted in the creation of Transcontinental and Western Air (TWA) in 1930, a title shortened to Trans World some 20 years later. The airline remained a domestic operator for many years, playing a large part in the development of the DC-2 and DC-3 types. After a similar involvement in the Constellation, TWA became an international carrier with routes extending worldwide. Its entry into the wide-bodied era came only a few months after rival Pan Am had introduced the 747, a type TWA also acquired together with TriStars. The airline became a publicly owned company in February 1984, but in 1985 52% of the shares were bought by a New York investor. During the next few years the company suffered financial difficulties and sought Chapter 11 bankruptcy protection. This ended in 1993 with the staff owning 45% of the shares. A second session under Chapter 11 soon followed from which TWA emerged once more in August 1995.

FLEET:

Boeing 747-131:	N53110, N53116, N93104, N93105, N93107, N93108, N93109,
Boeing 747-156:	N133TW, N134TW
Boeing 747-206B:	N306TW
Boeing 747-238B:	N614AR
Boeing 747-257B:	N303TW
Boeing 747-284B:	N305TW
Boeing 767-205ER:	N650TW, N651TW
Boeing 767-231ER:	N601TW, N602TW, N603TW, N604TW, N605TW, N606TW,
	N607TW, N608TW, N609TW, N610TW
Boeing 767-330ER:	N634TW, N692LF
Boeing 767-3Y0ER:	EI-CAM
L1011-385 TriStar 50:	N31019, N31023
L1011-385 TriStar 100:	N7036T, N31029, N31031
Also operated are Boeing 727s, DC-9s and MD80s.	

UK airport served: Gatwick.

Transaero Airlines (4J/TSO) — Russia
2nd Smolensky Pereulok, 121099 Moscow   Tel: (095) 241 11 90

Transaero was the first non-Aeroflot company allowed to operate passenger services in Russia, these starting in November 1991. The carrier's first international route linked Moscow with Tel Aviv, but others have subsequently been added to the network. It acquired its first Boeing 757 in 1994 which joined the 737s and 767s on the strength.

FLEET:

Boeing 737-236:	YL-BAA, YL-BAB, YL-BAC
Boeing 737-2C9:	EI-CLN, EI-CLO
Boeing 757-28A:	EI-CLM, EI-CLU, EI-CLV
Boeing 757-2Y0:	EI-CJX, EI-CJY
Boeing 757-2Q8:	EI-CLU, EI-CLV
Douglas DC-10-30:	-N140AA, N141AA, N142AA

UK airport served: Gatwick.

Transavia Airlines (HV/TRA) — Netherlands
PO Box 7777, NL-1118-ZM Schiphol Airport Centre   Tel: (20) 604 65 18

When the company was formed in 1965 it was known as Transavia (Limburg), later changing to Transavia Holland and finally to its present identity in 1986. The airline specialises in aircraft leasing and is also very much involved in IT charters for the Dutch travel industry. In recent years Transavia has also become a scheduled operator with services to Alicante, Faro, Gran Canaria, Heraklion, Gatwick, Malaga and Tenerife. It was also one of the first carriers to take advantage of the European liberalisation policy by operating services from

Above: **PH-HVJ — Boeing 737-3K2 of Transavia.**

bases not located in its home country. KLM is a majority shareholder but allows Transavia to retain its independence.

FLEET:

Boeing 737-33A: PH-HVI	
Boeing 737-3K2: PH-HVF, PH-HVG, PH-HVJ, PH-HVK, PH-HVM, PH-HVN, PH-HVT, PH-HVV, PH-TSX, PH-TSY, PH-TSZ	
Boeing 737-3L9: PH-TSW	
Boeing 737-3Q8: PH-TSX	
Boeing 737-3Y0: PH-TSU	
Boeing 757-2K2: PH-TKA, PH-TKB, PH-TKC, PH-TKD	

UK airport served: Gatwick.

TransLift Airways (T7/TLA) — Eire
26 Upper Fitzwilliam Street, Dublin 2 — Tel: (1) 662 18 88

The airline was founded in 1991 with DC-8s for long-haul cargo and passenger charters. Based at Shannon, the airline introduced a scheduled service to Los Angeles in 1993, but this was subsequently dropped. It also returned the DC-8s to the lessor in favour of some Airbus A320s, which are now used for European IT work. The airline is associated with All Leisure which has a 49% shareholding in the company.

FLEET:

Airbus A300B4: EI-CJK, EI-TLB

Airbus A320-231: EI-TLE, EI-TLF, EI-TLG, EI-TLI, EI-TLJ

UK airports served: Gatwick and Newcastle.

Transwede Airways (TQ/TWE) — Sweden
PO Box 135, S-19046 Stockholm-Arlanda — Tel: (8) 59 36 50 00

Formed in April 1985, Transwede operates scheduled services and IT passenger flights to the European holiday destinations. In the early 1990s the airline became associated with Sterling and Norway Airlines to form the Trans Nordic Group. It was intended to help the trio successfully compete with SAS and to inaugurate more low-cost scheduled services from Scandinavia. In the event, the venture was terminated, but Transwede remains in business with links to various destinations from Stockholm. The Gatwick schedule is operated under a code-sharing agreement with Finnair.

FLEET:

Boeing 757-236: SE-DUK

Boeing 757-2Y0: SE-DUL, SE-

Fokker 100: SE-DUC, SE-DUD, SE-DUE, SE-DUH, SE-DUI

McD Douglas MD83: SE-DLS, SE-DLU, SE-DLV, SE-DLX

McD Douglas MD87: SE-DHG, SE-DHI

UK airports served:

Tunis Air (TU/TAR) — Tunisia
Boulevard 7 Novembre, Tunis — Tel: (1) 70 01 00

Below: **TS-IMD — Airbus A320-211 of Tunis Air.**

The national carrier was founded by the government in 1948 with the help of private investors and Air France. Tunis Air was intended to develop the country's domestic network and to take over some of the short-haul routes from the French airline, so it was not long before the airline added Marseille, Nice and Paris to its coverage. In 1982 the first wide-bodied A300 arrived to take over the Cairo, Jeddah and Khartoum sectors in addition to the busy routes to France. Nowadays Tunis Air's aircraft are to be found at many European airports in addition to those in Africa and the Middle East.

FLEET:

Airbus A300B4-203: TS-IMA

Airbus A320-211: TS-IMB, TS-IMC, TS-IMD, TS-IME, TS-IMF, TS-IMG, TS-IMH, TS-IMI

Boeing 727-2H3: TS-JHN, TS-JHQ, TS-JHR, TS-JHS, TS-JHT, TS-JHU, TS-JHW

Boeing 737-2H3: TS-IOC, TS-IOD, TS-IOE, TS-IOF

Boeing 737-5H3: TS-IOG, TS-IOH, TS-IOI, TS-IOJ

UK airport served: Heathrow.

Turkish Airlines (TK/THY) — Turkey
Ataturk Airport, Yesilkoy, Istanbul 34830 — Tel: (212) 574 74 02

Above: TC-JDH — Boeing 737-4Y0 of Turkish Airlines.

Turkish State Airlines was formed in 1933 by the Ministry of Public Works to take over the running of the country's air transport operations. The airline's first route linked Istanbul with Ankara and was flown by Dragon Rapides. Recovery after the war was aided by the introduction of DC-3s which gave the carrier the opportunity to begin some winter flights towards the end of 1946. The present title was adopted in 1956 with the government by far the largest shareholder, although BOAC did possess a 6% holding at this point. By this time services ventured outside the boundaries of the country, with expansion speeded up with the arrival of five Viscounts in 1957. Subsequent modernisation programmes resulted in DC-9s, DC-10s, Boeing 707s and Boeing 727s carrying the company's livery until it became their turn to be replaced by the next generation of airliners. Airbus A310s were introduced, while the mainstay of the 1990s fleet became the Boeing 737-400 series. The airline's domestic subsidiary, THT, was integrated in 1993.

FLEET:

Airbus A310-203: TC-JCL, TC-JCM, TC-JCN, TC-JCO, TC-JCR, TC-JCS, TC-JCU	
Airbus A310-304: TC-JCV, TC-JCY, TC-JCZ, TC-JDA, TC-JDB, TC-JDC, TC-JDD	
Airbus A340-311: TC-JDJ, TC-JDK, TC-JDL, TC-JDM, TC-JDN	
Boeing 727-2F2: TC-JBF, TC-JCA, TC-JCB, TC-JCD	
Boeing 737-4Q8: TC-JDI, TC-JED, TC-JEE, TC-JEF, TC-JEG, TC-JEH, TC-JEI, TC-JEJ, TC-JEK, TC-JEL, TC-JEM, TC-JEN, TC-JEO, TC-JEP	
Boeing 737-4Y0: TC-JDE, TC-JDF, TC-JDG, TC-JDH, TC-JDT, TC-JDY, TC-JDZ, TC-JER, TC-JET, TC-JEU, TC-JEV, TC-JEY, TC-JEZ	
Boeing 737-42J: TC-JEA	
Boeing 737-5Y0: TC-JDU, TC-JDV	
Also operated are Avro RJ100s	

UK airports served: Heathrow and Stansted.

Ukraine International Airlines (PS/AUI) — Ukraine
Prospekt Pobedy 14, 252135 Kiev — Tel: (044) 216 67 58

The government-controlled airline was established in October 1992 as Air Ukraine International, but changed its name to avoid confusion with the domestic carrier, Air Ukraine. It also found that its two Boeing 737-400s provided too much capacity so these were replaced by two Series 200s in 1994. Schedules are flown to a range of European cities and are likely to be expanded as additional aircraft are acquired.

FLEET:

Boeing 737-247: UR-GAC	
Boeing 737-2T4: UR-GAD	
Boeing 737-3Y0: UR-GAE	

UK airport served: Gatwick.

United Airlines (UA/UAL) — USA

PO Box 66100, Chicago IL 60666   Tel: (708) 952 40 00

Established in 1934, the airline is now one of the world's largest with a route network serving 105 domestic and 39 international airports located in 30 countries. It expanded considerably in 1986 when it bought Pan Am's Pacific division, a transaction which included both aircraft and staff. Subsequently the airline added transatlantic schedules to its range of activities, using Heathrow as the UK gateway for a number of services to the US and for the European connecting flights operated with Boeing 727s. These have now ended following a co-operative agreement with Lufthansa.

FLEET:

Boeing 747-122: N4714U, N4716U, N4717U, N4718U, N4719U, N4720U, N4723U, N4724U, N4727U, N4728U, N4729U, N4732U, N4735U

Boeing 747-123: N153UA, N154UA, N155UA, N156UA, N157UA

Boeing 747-222B: N151UA, N152UA

Boeing 747-238B: N158UA, N159UA, N160UA, N161UA, N163UA, N164UA, N165UA

Boeing 747-422: N171UA, N172UA, N173UA, N174UA, N175UA, N176UA, N177UA, N178UA, N179UA, N180UA, N181UA, N182UA, N183UA, N184UA, N185UA, N186UA, N187UA, N188UA, N189UA, N190UA, N191UA, N192UA, N193UA, N194UA, N195UA

Boeing 747-451: N105UA, N106UA

Boeing 767-222ER: N601UA, N602UA, N603UA, N604UA, N605UA, N606UA, N607UA, N608UA, N609UA, N610UA, N611UA

Boeing 767-322ER: N641UA, N642UA, N643UA, N644UA, N645UA, N646UA, N647UA, N648UA, N649UA, N650UA, N651UA, N652UA, N653UA, N654UA, N655UA, N656UA, N657UA, N658UA, N659UA, N660UA, N661UA, N662UA, N663UA

Boeing 777-222: N766UA, N767UA, N768UA, N769UA, N770UA, N771UA, N772UA, N773UA, N774UA, N775UA, N776UA, N777UA, N778UA, N779UA, N780UA, N781UA, N782UA, N783UA, N784UA, N785UA, N786UA, N787UA, N788UA

Also operated are Airbus A320s, Boeing 727/737/757s and DC-10s.

UK airport served: Heathrow.

United Parcel Service (5X/UPS) — USA

1400 North Hurstbourne Parkway, Louisville, KY 40223   Tel: (502) 329 65 00

Until the mid-1980s UPS used the equipment of other carriers for its extensive overnight parcels delivery services to 185 countries and territories. In 1988 the company formed its own airline and now serves more points in the US than any

Above: **N805UP — Douglas DC-8-73AF of United Parcel Services.** *A. S. Wright*

other carrier, with European destinations added in 1985.

FLEET:

Boeing 747-121F: N681UP, N682UP, N683UP
Boeing 747-123F: N672UP, N673UP, N674UP, N675UP, N676UP, N677UP
Boeing 767-34AFER: N301UP, N302UP, N303UP, N304UP, N305UP, N306UP, N307UP, N308UP, N309UP, N310UP, N311UP, N312UP, N313UP, N314UP, N315UP
Douglas DC-8-73AF: N801UP, N802UP, N803UP, N804UP, N805UP, N806UP, N807UP, N808UP, N809UP, N810UP, N811UP, N812UP, N813UP, N814UP, N815UP, N816UP, N818UP, N819UP, N836UP, N840UP, N851UP, N852UP, N866UP, N867UP, N868UP, N874UP, N880UP, N894UP

UK airport served: East Midlands.

Uzbekistan Airways (HY/UZB)   Uzbekistan
41 Ulitsa Proletarskaya, Tashkent 700061   Tel: (3712) 33 18 85

Founded in 1992 from the previous Aeroflot division, the airline has progressed well with its expansion plans. These centre around Western-built equipment, with a pair of Airbus A310s already employed on the busier long-haul routes to Europe and the Middle East.

FLEET:

Airbus A310-324: F-OGQY, F-OGQZ

Boeing 757-23P: UK-75700

Boeing 767-35PER: UK-76701, UK-76702

Ilyushin IL-62: UK-86659, UK-86694

Ilyushin IL-62M: UK-86569, UK-86573, UK-86574, UK-86575, UK-86576, UK-86577, UK-86578, UK-86579

Also operated An-24, IL-76/86/114, Tu-154B and Yak-40.

UK airports served: Heathrow and Manchester.

Above: UK-86578 — Ilyushin IL-62M of Uzbekistan Airways.

Varig (RG/VRG)   Brazil
Avenue Almirante Silvio de Noronha 365,
CEP 20021 Rio de Janeiro   Tel: (21) 272 50 00

From humble beginnings in 1927, Varig has progressed to become South America's largest carrier. Along the way it has absorbed a number of other airlines, both small and large, one in the latter category being Panair do Brasil, a substantial but failed international operator. The present-day network includes some 44 domestic and 38 international destinations in Africa, Asia, Central and South America, Europe and North America. Financial problems in 1994 resulted in Varig cancelling aircraft orders, ceasing uneconomic services, cutting staff numbers and generally renegotiating leases.

FLEET:

Boeing 767-241ER: PP-VNN, PP-VNO, PP-VNP, PP-VNQ, PP-VNR, PP-VNS

Boeing 767-341ER: PP-VOI, PP-VOJ, PP-VOK, PP-VOL

McD Douglas MD11: PP-VOP, PP-VOQ, PP-VPJ, PP-VPK, PP-VPL, PP-VPM

UK airport served: Heathrow.

Viasa (VA/VIA)   Venezuela

Plaza Morelos, Avenida Sur 25,
Los Caobos, Caracas 105   Tel: (2) 576 04 11

The government decided to create a carrier to take over the responsibility for
international flights in 1961. It reached an agreement with KLM to provide a DC-8
for the proposed transatlantic route and also to act as European agent. A few
months after the Amsterdam schedule was started, Viasa began a New York link
using its own equipment for the first time. The network has subsequently been
expanded to include a number of cities in Europe and the Americas, while charters
are operated to Toronto and Vancouver during the Canadian winter season.

FLEET:

Douglas DC-10-30: YV-134C, YV-135C, YV-136C, YV-137C, YV-138C, YV-139C

Also operated are Boeing 727.

UK airport served: Heathrow.

Virgin Atlantic Airways (VS/VIR)   United Kingdom

Ashdown House, High Street, Crawley, West Sussex   Tel: (01293) 562345

British Atlantic Airways was formed in 1982 with the intention of operating
passenger services between London and New York. However, during the period
prior to the inaugural flight in 1984, the company was acquired by the Virgin
Record Group with the result that the name was changed to Virgin Atlantic
Airways. It also meant that instead of the luxury cabin originally planned, the
new management opted for low-cost flights aimed at a wider range of
travellers. For a time feeder services were operated from Maastricht in the
Netherlands, but although good passenger loads were obtained, only a small
percentage were actually bound for New York. It was found that sufficient
traffic was generated at Gatwick anyway, so the Dutch connection was
dropped. The Boeing 747 fleet has gradually expanded as new routes have
been added, while the first Airbus A340 was introduced in 1994. Virgin now
flies from both Gatwick and Heathrow to a number of US destinations together
with Tokyo and Hong Kong. The airline also had a franchise agreement with
City Jet which operates a London City–Dublin schedule, while an Athens route
was maintained in 1994 under a similar scheme by South East European
Airlines. In April 1996, Virgin acquired a 90% share of EuroBelgian Airlines to
become Virgin European Express.

FLEET:

Airbus A320-231: G-OUZO

Airbus A340-311: G-VAEL, G-VBUS, G-VFLY, G-VSKY, G-VSUN, G-

Boeing 747-123: G-VMIA

Boeing 747-238B: G-VJFK, G-VLAX

Boeing 747-243B: G-VGIN

Boeing 747-283B: G-VOYG

Boeing 747-287B: G-VBIG, G-VIRG

Boeing 747-4Q8: G-VFAB, G-VHOT

Above: G-VLAX — Boeing 747-238B of Virgin Atlantic Airways.

UK airports served: Gatwick and Heathrow.

Virgin European Express — Belgium
See EuroBelgian Airlines

Viva Air (FV/VIV) — Spain
Camino de la Escollera 4, E-07012 Palma — Tel: (71) 21 91 00

The airline was formed in February 1988 by Iberia and Lufthansa to operate passenger services within Europe. It is now almost wholly owned by the Spanish flag carrier which has now taken back most of the schedules, leaving Viva with more scope to operate ITs for various tour companies.

FLEET:

Boeing 737-3K9: EC-ELY

Boeing 737-36E: EC-FFN, EC-FHR, EC-FLF, EC-FLG, EC-GAP, EC-GBU, EC-GGE, EC-GGZ

UK airports served: Birmingham, Edinburgh, Gatwick, Glasgow, Manchester, Newcastle and Stansted.

Above: **EC-FLF — Boeing 737-36E of Viva Air.**

VLM (VG/VLM)   Belgium
Antwerp Airport, B-2100 Deurne   Tel: (3) 230 90 00

The Belgian airline began a four-times daily scheduled service between its
Antwerp base and London City in May 1993. In the following year Rotterdam
was added to the coverage following the demise of Flexair, VLM also becoming
the first foreign airline to operate a UK domestic scheduled service when it
introduced a twice-daily London City route. Unfortunately, the latter did not
receive sufficient support so it was ceased at the end of the year. A four-times
daily link between London City and the new Dusseldorf Express airport at
Monchengladbach was started in April 1996.

FLEET:

Fokker 50: OO-VLE, OO-VLJ, OO-VLK, OO-VLM, OO-VLN

UK airport served: London City.

Above: **OO-VLN — Fokker 50 of VLM.**

World Airlines (W2)   United Kingdom
14A Ganton Street, London   Tel: (0171) 439 4539

World Airlines became the first carrier to be based at London City Airport, from
where it plans to operate scheduled services to a number of European
destinations. The first of these was launched on 13 May 1996 to link the
docklands airport with Amsterdam four-times daily with a BAe 146-200. A
second machine was delivered in mid-summer, in preparation for a route to
Copenhagen to be added to the coverage. It was also intended to operate
regular flights at weekends for the leisure market, leaving weekdays to
concentrate upon the needs of the business community. Unfortunately World
was forced to suspend all operations in early October, but hopes to restart as
soon as possible.

FLEET:

BAe 146-200: G-WLCY, G-OWLD

UK airport served: London City

World Airways (WO/WOA)   USA
13873 Park Centre Road, Herndon, Va 22071   Tel: (703) 834 92 00

World was founded in 1948 to operate passenger and freight charters. The
airline moved into the scheduled market in 1979 when it began low-cost
intercontinental services in the US. Two years later in 1981, routes to Honolulu,
London and Frankfurt were launched. By the mid-1980s World was becoming
unprofitable, so in an attempt to reverse the trend, the management decided
to cease all schedules in September 1986. After a lengthy period, passenger
operations were restarted in March 1993 and have since been increased to

Israeli and South African destinations, while interest has been shown in the UK market. World also plans to commence round-the-world cargo flights.

FLEET:

Douglas DC-10-30: N107WA, N117WA

McD Douglas MD11: N271WA, N272WA, N273WA, N274WA, N275WA, N276WA, N277WA, N278WA, N280WA

UK airports served: Belfast and Manchester.

Yemenia (IY/IYE) — Yemen
PO Box 6006, Sana'a, Yemen — Tel: (1) 23 23 80

Founded as Yemen Airlines in 1963, nationalisation in 1972 brought a change of name and reorganisation to the company. The amalgamation of North and South Yemen in 1990 was also responsible for a merger of Yemen Airways with Alyemda two years later. The carrier now flies both domestic and international schedules, the latter to Europe, the Middle East and Asia.

FLEET:

Airbus A310-304: F-ODSV

Airbus A310-325: 7O-, 7O-

Boeing 727-2N8: 7O-ACV, 7O-ACW, 7O-ACX, 7O-ACY, 7O-ADA

Ilyushin IL-76TD: 7O-ADF, 7O-ADG, 7O-ADH

UK airports served: Gatwick and Stansted (freight).